# Snowdonia

The Sychnant pass

# Snowdonia's landscape

John Whittow

Illustrations by Duncan McCrae, John Whittow
and Helen Walshaw

London
GEORGE ALLEN & UNWIN
Boston          Sydney

**George Allen & Unwin (Publishers) Ltd,**
**40 Museum Street, London WC1A 1LU, UK**

George Allen & Unwin (Publishers) Ltd,
Park Lane, Hemel Hempstead, Herts HP2 4TE, UK

Allen & Unwin Inc.,
9 Winchester Terrace, Winchester, Mass 01890, USA

George Allen & Unwin Australia Pty Ltd,
8 Napier Street, North Sydney, NSW 2060, Australia


First published in 1985

ISSN 0265–3117

Sketch maps on pp. 42, 52, 66, 148 and 159 based in part on Ordnance
Survey mapping: Crown Copyright reserved.

**British Library Cataloguing in Publication Data**

Whittow, John
    Snowdonia's landscape. – (Unwin landscape
guides, ISSN 0265–3117; 4)
1. Snowdonia (Wales) – Description and travel
I. Title
914.29'25      DA740.S6
ISBN 0–04–551097–0

Set in 9 on 10 point Palatino by Nene Phototypesetters, Northampton
and printed in Great Britain by Richard Clay (The Chaucer Press) Ltd,
Bungay, Suffolk

# Contents

*To my parents, who introduced me to the grandeur of Snowdonia*

# Introduction: the lure of Snowdonia

The northern mountainlands of Wales have been the natural play-ground for millions of folk from Merseyside, Manchester and the Midlands for more than a century, making it a landscape familiar to countless people. Yet this grey rocky fortress, moated by the Conwy Valley in the east and the estuaries of Traeth Mawr and Traeth Bach in the south had been reluctant to surrender its secrets for centuries until the early 19th century roads and railways penetrated its misty recesses. The invading Romans and 13th century English armies found the mountain fastnesses to be both inhospitable and almost inaccessible. The virtually trackless uplands and heavy rainfall made early visitors fearful of venturing far from the narrow coastal plains. The spectacular cliffs, waterfalls, gorges and dizzy summits which now excite admiration were virtually unknown until intrepid pioneers in the late 18th and early-19th centuries brought back descriptions and drawings, as if from darkest Africa. These early travellers, such as Dr Johnson and George Borrow, were forced to walk or ride on horseback into the so-called wilderness, for it was not until Thomas Telford's roads and Robert Stephenson's railways had 'opened up' North Wales that English visitors began to arrive in force. Today, the numbers have increased so greatly, that the landscape is beginning to suffer at particularly popular spots such as Snowdon and Cwm Idwal, and footpath erosion is now one of the National Park Authority's greatest problems.

It must be remembered that Snowdonia is not an uninhabited wilderness; it is the homeland of a sturdy breed of Celts whose culture and language have survived gradual Anglicization over the centuries. This is their land, a land of hill farmers, quarrymen and fishermen, who have fought to make their livelihoods from a bleak and harsh upland environment. It is they who have fashioned nature's handiwork into the traditional landscapes which you see today and which tempt you to return so frequently.

The Welsh are pleased and proud that you are able to admire their scenery and learn something of their heritage. In this way tourism has developed into the most important source of income for many of the inhabitants of this remarkable region.

Most tourists stay at the well known coastal resorts of Llandudno, Conwy, Penmaenmawr, Llanfairfechan, Bangor, Nefyn, Criccieth, and Porthmadog, all within sight of the mountainland. Thus, this guide is written as though you were setting off from these perimeter settlements. Many more travellers, campers, caravanners, walkers and climbers stay within the uplands themselves at such idyllic centres as Betws-y-Coed and Beddgelert, which feature regularly in the itineraries. The larger towns of the mountains, such as Bethesda, Llanberis and Blaenau Ffestiniog have grown with the slate industry, but because they still offer something of fascinating difference in their grizzled fabrics they too are now becoming tourist attractions in their own right. There are numerous camping and caravan sites both within Snowdonia and along its surrounding coasts (see Appendix for details).

Snowdonia is attractive at all seasons but the Easter holidays and high summer months are especially popular. At these times resorts may be crowded and the footpaths, roads and car parks congested. So, if you can, why not try late spring or early autumn: the former gives you a riot of rhododendrons, verdant pastures, newly born lambs, daffodils and rain-washed skies, while the latter offers autumnal colours, the first dusting of snow on the hill tops, the long, sharp evening shadows of the peaks across the purple heather moors, and in the morning the mist-filled valleys. These are neglected seasons, but usually times of tranquillity, when you are able to stand and admire the magnificent mountain vistas, or seek solitude in the hidden valleys and woodlands. The walks and drives in this guide are intended to explain the landscapes which you are exploring and add something to your enjoyment and understanding of the lure of Snowdonia.

*Key to symbols*

| | |
|---|---|
| 🍵 | cafe |
| 🅿 | car park |
| 🏰 | castle, abbey, stately home, etc. |
| 🚗 | motor route |
| **M** | museum, gallery, exhibition, etc. |
| PO | post office |
| ⊕ | public house |
| 🏪 | shop |
| [Conwy >] | signpost |
| ℘ | telephone |
| **wc** | toilet |
| **ℹ** | tourist information |
| ⋇ | viewpoint |
| 🚶 | walking route |

In Snowdonia most signs are written in both Welsh and English but in case they are in Welsh only the following may be useful:

| | |
|---|---|
| amserlen | timetable |
| cyfleustrau | toilets |
| dim parcio | no parking |
| dynion | men |
| maes parcio | car parking |
| merched | ladies |
| rheilffordd | railway |
| sengl | single (fare) |
| dwy ffordd | return (fare) |

# PART 1   BACKGROUND

# The landscape unfolds

Most people have an intuitive feeling for landscape – they know what they like and dislike, but are often hard pressed to give reasons for their choice. In recent years, attempts have been made to explain these preferences in terms of shape, colour, texture and proportion, but results are mainly inconclusive. An enjoyment of landscape is a personal thing. It may evoke pleasant memories or offer potential experiences. What one person sees in a landscape may be quite different from that seen by another. An artist, an engineer, a farmer or a soldier will probably all look for different attributes and have different preferences. This book is written for the tourist who comes for enjoyment and exercise. By explaining the different facets of the scenery it is hoped that the visitor's experience will be enhanced. Most people are inquisitive and they generally ask why things happen and what makes the scenery so different from place to place. It will be shown how the landscape of Snowdonia has evolved over millions of years. Nature has provided the framework and man has simply added the thinnest of veneers, the 'human touch', that fundamental skin of the Earth that manifests itself in the field patterns, villages, paths, roads and railways.

In 1951 the Snowdonia National Park became the third of our heritage landscapes to be so designated (after the Peak District and Lake District). As such it had to be . . . 'an extensive area of beautiful and relatively wild country in which . . . (a) the characteristic landscape beauty is strictly preserved, (b) access and facilities for public open-air enjoyment are amply provided, (c) wildlife, and buildings and places of architectural and historic interest are suitably protected, while (d) established farming use is effectively main-tained.' This was the definition of the National Parks and Access to the Countryside Act, 1949. The aims are clear but it is equally apparent that this is a living, working landscape, not a fossilised museum piece. Only 30 per cent of the land is 'public' and much of that is devoted to forestry, water resources and electricity gener-ation. But it is this dynamic element which often provides the interest for the tourist who can witness the many ways in which man has worked with nature to create such a fascinating tapestry. Not all the 838 square miles of the park will be covered in this volume, only the 700 square miles in the north which comprise the real Snowdonia.

If you could view it from a plane you would see how compact the massif is: 35 miles (56 km) from Conwy in the north-east to Yr Eifl in the south-west and a mere 20 miles (32 km) between the Menai Strait in the north and Trawsfynydd Lake in the south. You would also see how the brown peaty moorlands are punctuated with grey rocky islands (the peaks) and seamed by bright-green corridors where river valleys provide shelter and fertile soils for both woodland and farmland. Here and there a long silvery valley lake reflects the light, while a scatter of tiny jewel-like flashes pinpoint the hidden mountain lakes in their dark craggy hollows. To the north the bright check tablecloth of Anglesey's corn and pastureland drapes the horizon; eastwards the less ordered mosaic of plateau farmlands marches into Clwyd; the boggy southern moorlands extend the National Park southwards to the crags of Cader Idris, while the probing finger of the Llyn Peninsula with its knuckly western hills, completes the enclosing framework.

Although the Irish Sea wraps round three sides of Snowdonia, its waves are attacking the mountains only in the far west (Yr Eifl) and the north-east (near Conwy). Elsewhere the natural bulwark of Anglesey or the artificial creations of man (near Porthmadog) have apparently excluded the fretting action of the sea. But the sea is never far away, and coastal routes dominate the scene because these peripheral plains still offer the best means of access. So it is with the towns: with few exceptions the major urban settlements are coastal, fringing the bare central massif with a rash of stone, slate, bricks, mortar, steel and concrete. Here, on the perimeter, the works of man are in the ascendant; in the mountainland, however, nature's handiwork takes precedence, with a few notable exceptions. Yet there is no clear demarcation line. Along the few exposed shores, for example, the ocean still continues its inexorable arithmetic, subtracting land from the headlands and adding it to the bays. In the rugged uplands the farmer grapples with his sheep runs and his stone walls, the forester with his trees and the engineer with his pylons and pipelines. It is this interaction of human and physical factors which creates the landscape, and you can now begin to appreciate why landscape is dynamic – it changes not only from place to place and through the seasons but with the passage of time. By and large nature works slowly, but man appears always to be in a hurry, sometimes making mistakes and triggering a disastrous spasm in the natural order of things. The natural framework of Snowdonia has taken more than 500 million years to evolve, while human activity has made a significant impact only in the past 1000 years. It is when you stop to ponder these things that you can begin to understand the scale of events and the rates at which changes have occurred.

## Once upon a time

Although the geologist tells us that there is no semblance of a beginning, every story has to have a starting point. The preface to Snowdonia's story book starts almost 600 million years ago, when a continent of ancient rocks was split apart by earth movements, thereby allowing the oceans to flood into the intervening gap. Only fragments of this ancient continent have survived, in Anglesey, western Llyn and the ridge upon which Bangor now stands. The slow forces of wind, rain and frost then, as now, would have chipped slowly away at the continent, splintering the summits and moving the debris slowly down to the rivers and thence to the sea. This is the process that geologists term 'erosion' and it is a fundamental process of nature. It is quite inevitable and virtually impossible to halt on anything more than a local scale. It operates at different speeds according to the climate, slowing down in desert areas, speeding up when glaciers appear. The most significant tool, however, has always been running water, manifesting itself as a stream or river, for this is the major agent of transport, a type of conveyor belt, shifting material from the uplands down to the lowlands. This is one of the reasons why mountains are worn down and estuaries are silted up. If you have experienced typical Snowdonian weather, of heavy rain and streaming slopes, you will soon understand how water can carry away loose debris. It is the rainwater that imperceptibly rots the rock to create the soil which in places mantles the bare rock. Only when it becomes waterlogged does it tear away from the hillside as a landslip. Nevertheless, soil is always on the move down the hillslopes, ending up in the streams from whence it moves down to the sea. But don't be under the illusion that the Welsh climate has always caused processes like this. For lengthy periods in the millions of years of its history, North Wales has sometimes experienced desert conditions, while at other times it lay beneath overwhelming ice sheets; for even longer spans it was submerged beneath far-spreading tropical oceans. Occasionally, its relatively quiet environments were torn with volcanic eruptions when towering vents spewed vast lava flows across the land or piled great thicknesses of ash and pumice on to the ocean floor, where they buried those sands and muds which had been brought down by rivers, were carried offshore by submarine currents and were finally converted into sandstones, shales and mudstones. Between these times the crustal surface rose and fell, convulsed by the Earth's internal spasms, wracked by earthquakes, bent, buckled and fractured by the restless shifting of the continents as they jostled for position across the globe. It is precisely because the continents change their position that different climates have prevailed at any one location during the various chapters of Earth's long history. Thus, each chapter (or period of geological time) may differ from the next and the rocks beneath your feet reflect these differences. The tropical forests helped build Britain's coalfields, the warm coral seas produced many of its limestones, its ice sheets gave thicknesses of glacial rubbish we now call boulder clay. You may well ask if there is any order in this apparent chaos? Can the chapters of this Earth history book be easily read?

## Ocean deep and mountain high

Start chapter one by considering a single layer of mud on the ocean floor (or, if you like, a single page of the Earth history book). As more layers of sediment accumulate the mud becomes buried, gradually compressed and turned into a thin sheet of rock called 'mudstone'. All this takes millions of years and during this time the climate changes. The neighbouring continent has now become a desert from which sand grains and gravels reach the sea, carried down the desert valleys by occasional flash floods. The result is to create different

types of rocks, those from the deserts producing sandstones and pebbly gritstones which buried the existing layered mudstones on the ocean floor. The mudstones were eventually to become the well known Welsh slates while the pebbly sandstones form part of the hard Harlech gritstones of southern Snowdonia. The middle of chapter one is reached when the sea retreated and the rock layers were uplifted, tilted and eroded, as if a wilful child had crumpled and torn the early pages of the book.

One hundred million years elapsed before there was another invasion of the sea. Instead of a desert sea, the new ocean was teeming with wildlife, and fewer sandy layers were deposited among the muds. But it was also a period of crustal unease, with chains of volcanic islands pouring forth their glowing lavas and belching out clouds of ash. Enormous explosions rent the sea bed and pulverised the older volcanic rocks into fragments, throwing them high into the air before they rained down to become interbedded with the newer lavas. Between these fiery episodes the muds continued to accumulate, eventually building a gigantic layer cake of sedimentary and igneous (i.e. fire-formed) rocks. The thousands of feet of the Snowdonian Volcanics, as they have since been termed, make up the majority of the exposed rocks in the modern mountainland and it is to these that the rugged grandeur of Snowdonia can be attributed. Most of the crags and jagged summits are built from such volcanic rocks. Sometimes the lava flows took place at depth, never reaching the surface, but instead forcing their way between the bedded rocks to form sheets of dolerite and basalt called 'sills'. These are particularly hard rocks which, when exposed at the surface by erosion, invariably create cliffs and steep ridges in the landscape. The first chapter closes about 400 million years ago with an enormous upheaval of the ocean floor rocks as two continents collided. The bedded rocks were crushed into concertina-like folds, the mudstones squeezed into slates, and all were eventually fractured and overturned by the continuing pressure. The upfolds ('anticlines') and downfolds ('synclines') were then hoisted bodily by the deep crustal convulsion to form a gigantic mountain chain stretching from Ireland and Wales to Scotland. Although these Himalayan-like peaks have long since been worn down to mere stumps, the roots of their immense primeval folds still survive – the synclinal summit of Snowdon and the downfold of the Devil's Kitchen are two of the best known.

It was this lengthy period which also witnessed upwelling of chemical fluids from the deep-seated molten rocks, fluids which were to create the valuable metal deposits of the mountainland.

Throughout the succeeding middle chapters of the Earth history book (which together span another 350 million years), the slow accumulation of mudstones, sandstones and limestones continued virtually unbroken throughout Wales. Yet in Snowdonia today there is no record of these later rocks, as if hundreds of pages have been forcibly removed from the middle of the book. The reason is not far to

(Opposite) **Snowdonia 500 million years ago**

seek: the successive periods of erosion have completely obliterated the topmost layers of the highland massif, stripping them away to reveal the buried bones of the oldest rocks. Thus, it is impossible to do more than speculate whether Snowdonia was once graced with white Carboniferous Limestone, like that at Llandudno, or bright red Old Red Sandstone, similar to that on nearby Anglesey. Perhaps there were Coal Measures too, for coal was once mined on Anglesey, not far from the Menai Strait. While rain, frost and landslide wore down the surface, enormous subterranean forces were at work heaving the Snowdonian region into a dome upon which rivers flowed radially outwards. It was this slow upheaval which initiated the high massif and it was the work of rivers that created the deep wrinkles on its ancient countenance.

The upheaval also caused cracks ('faults') in the crustal rocks to move, sometimes with such rapidity that they produced an earthquake. They have moved sporadically ever since. Nothing comparable to the Californian or Japanese 'quakes has disturbed modern Snowdonia, although quite severe tremors have been recorded on four known occasions, 1690, 1852, 1903 and 1984. The most recent (19 July 1984) caused damage to numerous buildings between Conwy and the Llyn Peninsula and led to the closure of a church at Porth Dinorwig. It was caused by a sudden movement along a fault which crosses the Llyn Peninsula and proved to be one of Britain's most powerful earthquakes since records began.

# The world of ice

Even if so many of the intermediate 'pages' are missing from Snowdonia's story book, one of its concluding chapters is intact and it is also one of the most important, so far as the scenery is concerned. A mere 2 million years ago the climate changed once more as North Wales became gripped within the frozen embrace of the Ice Age. The arctic climate set to work on the dome-shaped upland where smooth slopes and slowly flowing rivers prevailed. The crustal spasms which had raised the European Alps had simply continued the uplift of the North Welsh massif, so that its maximum elevation had been achieved before the refrigeration set in. Prior to the Ice Age, thick layers of soil would have mantled the solid rock and moved only slowly down into the shallow river valleys. As much of the world's moisture became 'locked-up' in the polar ice caps, so the sea level gradually fell. The North Wales coastline would have advanced many miles seaward of its present position, thereby extending its coastal plains well beyond the Llyn Peninsula and Anglesey (which had yet to become an island).

As the cold weather set in, vegetation became more stunted and tundra-like, bare grasslands would have clothed the land as the winter snows began to linger in the hollows. Shielded from the sunshine, the hollows which faced north-east were the most favoured sites for the snow patches to accumulate, eventually to grow

(Opposite) **The downfold of the Devil's Kitchen cliffs, Idwal**

into tiny glaciers. The majority of Snowdonia's glacial hollows face between north and east, as is well shown in the valley of Nant Ffrancon. As the climate further deteriorated these glaciers expanded and moved forward out of their high basins before joining forces on the valley floors. These valley glaciers themselves became thicker as they in turn amalgamated until their valleys were brimming full. Ice then spilled outwards over gaps in the ridges in an attempt to move away from the congested mountainland, eventually emerging as great coalescing ice tongues onto the surrounding lowlands. It is thought that during many of the coldest episodes of the Ice Age, ice sheets in North Wales were thick enough to bury even the highest peaks, so that the landscape resembled not so much the modern Alps but more the white wilderness of Antarctica or Greenland. From the north, fresh ice sheets drove down the now dried out basin of the Irish Sea, pushing right over Anglesey and Llyn but unable to penetrate Snowdonia because of its own thick ice cap.

All the ice sheets and mountain glaciers picked and plucked at the surface, sweeping away the soil mantle and quarrying the newly exposed rocks, themselves weakened by the destructive action of frost. It was the broken lumps of rock carried in the base of the ice that had such severe effects on Snowdonia's scenery. So abrasive were these 'hobnailed' glaciers that they scooped out the pre-glacial hollows into armchair-shaped recesses, known in Welsh as 'cwms', and gouged out valleys into glacial troughs by their remorseless grinding action. Few were the rocky obstacles that could withstand such a pounding, although some of the tougher igneous rocks stood proud by comparison with their sedimentary neighbours. The highest summits, occasionally standing above the ice sheets, were themselves attacked unmercifully by frost, which slowly converted them into little more than heaps of shattered rock, much of which slid down their slopes in the form of 'screes'. Where the cwms were eaten back into the heart of the mountain by the voracious glaciers, so the rounded peaks were sculptured into pyramids and cones, while ridges were chiselled into knife edges, of which Crib Goch is a spectacular example.

By the time the Ice Age had waned the rolling mountainland had been remarkably transformed: cwms pockmarked the bare slopes like bomb craters; the ends of gentle ridges now plunged vertically into the glacially enlarged valleys; lakes now appeared where none had existed before; ice-transported blocks teetered precariously on steep hill slopes; thick layers of boulder clay swamped the lowland margins and heaps of glacial boulders were strewn like giant sandcastles around the rocky hollows and deeply cut mountain passes. Such was the obstacle course left for mankind to colonise, but first the soil and vegetation had to regain a toehold in this barren and bleak wilderness. Slowly the wind, rain and seasonal frost were able to renew their interminable tasks of moulding the battered and bruised landscape – smoothing off here, infilling there – converting

(Opposite) **The glacially gouged hollow of Cwm Ffynnon**

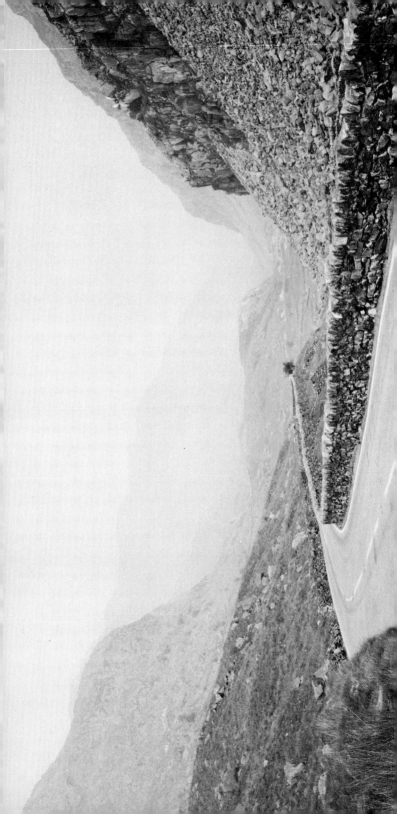

the starkness into something more amenable to the regeneration of forests and grasslands. But so far these ameliorating agencies have not had much time – a mere 10 000 years. Thus, Snowdonia had barely been able to hide its battle scars before the last chapter of its story book was reached.

## The human touch

Early man's choice of habitation was governed largely by such factors as slope steepness, shelter from prevailing winds, soil fertility, land drainage, water supply and changing forest cover. By the time Snowdonia's first human colonisers arrived, some 2000 years ago, its valleys had accumulated sufficient depth of soil to support a thick growth of forest up to elevations of some 1500 feet (457 m). Oak was the dominant tree (there are a few surviving patches even today) with alder on the marshy places and birch on the thinner, stonier soils. This left only the windswept summits of the high central mountains or the bare coastal hills as places suitable for settlement, since the earliest arrivals had only stone tools, incapable of effective forest clearance without the additional help of fire, Nonetheless, these vigorous Stone Age folk, who arrived by sea, settled in tiny peripheral hill villages in the Llyn Peninsula and in the northern hills between Conwy and Penmaenmawr where they discovered hard, igneous rocks which they could chip and polish into excellent tools. On the cliffs behind Penmaenmawr, for instance, an axe factory exported its implements all over southern Britain. In addition, these Stone Age peoples were among the earliest to master the art of pottery making, permanent house building and, more importantly, they were able to domesticate livestock and grow grain, thus becoming Britain's first real farmers. But in these stony, inhospitable environments on windy hilltops their fields could have been compared only with present-day allotments, while modern farmers would barely recognise their scrawny sheep and cattle.

Some 500 years later a new wave of people with rudimentary bronze tools subdued the hardy Stone Age population and took control of their villages. Their two cultures gradually fused, but the newcomers brought with them a practice of cremating their dead and burying their remains (surrounded with bronze ornaments) within substantial piles of earth, known as 'tumuli'. Examples can still be found, scattered around Snowdonia's peripheral slopes, especially those of the Conwy Valley, the islands of the Glaslyn estuary and the neck of the Llyn Peninsula. The central mountainland at first remained virtually impassable because of its precipices and un-broken valley woodlands, but a change of climate was occurring, bringing drier conditions, so that the marshy valleys and alder swamps became less formidable. The sheltered sandy estuaries of Traeth Mawr and Traeth Bach at that time became an important distributing centre where trade routes came together. Coastal

(Opposite) **The U-shaped trough of the Llanberis Pass: note the ice-steepened spurs and the screes (on the right)**

shipping routes from the Mediterranean, Ireland (where gold had been discovered) and northern Europe converged here to link up with mountain trackways. It is not surprising, therefore, that with the availability of bronze implements the coastal settlers at last began to make inroads into the forested mountain valleys. Bronze Age finds have been made inland at Capel Curig, Trefriw, Dolwyddelan, Beddgelert and even on the slopes of Carnedd Llewelyn. But a change back to wet, stormy weather brought a fresh tangle of undergrowth to the valleys, restricting settlement sites largely to the well drained but sheltered hanging valleys, the lower cwms and the coastal foothills, places like Nant Gwynant, Cwm Pennant and Conwy Mountain.

A further wave of invaders began pushing into North Wales between 500 and 300 BC. Not only were these the first Celtic settlers, introducing the Welsh language and the Druid religion to the mountainland, but they brought with them invaluable iron tools, capable of extensive forest clearance. These so-called Iron Age peoples were also skilled in building and it is they who constructed the great stone and earth fortresses on the peripheral hill summits, such as Pen-y-Gaer above Dolgarrog, Maes-y-Gaer overlooking Aber, Castell Caer Leion on Conwy Mountain, Tre'r Ceiri on Yr Eifl and Dinas Emrys commanding the entrance to Nant Gwynant. You will see all of these on your walks and realise how they were situated on spurs of the lower hills where they could command extensive views of coastline and valley alike. For these were troubled times and the local farming families made sure that they had a place of refuge in times of attack. Archaeologists have demonstrated that many of the Iron Age hillforts became permanently settled and were even rebuilt and strengthened by the Romans who may have co-operated with the Celtic hill farmers in this stormy corner of their far-flung empire. By then the Welsh place names had been firmly established and have survived until the present day.

It took the Romans a mere seven years (71–8 AD) to conquer Snowdonia, from their legionary fortress at Deva (now Chester). They achieved it by building two auxiliary fortresses, one on the north coast, commanding the Menai Strait (Segontium, now Caernarfon), the other inland at Tomen-y-mur, now overlooking Trawsfynydd Nuclear Power Station. These were linked with paved roads, like that over Bwlch-y-Ddeufaen, and patrolled from smaller forts at Canovium, guarding a ford in the Conwy Valley, and Caer Llugwy, next to the Swallow Falls. It was the siting of these military outposts on the valley floors that gave the initial impetus to the Romano-British population to leave their hilltops and make permanent settlements in the valley clearings. From there they would barter wool, skins, corn and other produce at the fortress gates, finally moving within the walls as the Romans withdrew from North Wales before 400 AD. Thus, the first true native townsfolk became established at Caernarfon.

(Opposite) **Bare coastal hills above Penmaenmawr where the earliest prehistoric settlers made their homes**

The following list is a selection of Welsh place names that will help to explain their derivation and give you a clearer understanding of the landscape. The recommended singular form is given first, the plural form (where appropriate) next.

*aber*   estuary, river confluence
*afon*   river
*allt*   hillside (usually wooded), cliff
*bach (fach)*   small, little
*betws*   church, chapel
*bron*, pl. *bronnydd*   rounded hillside
*bryn*, pl. *bryniau*   hill
*bwlch (fwlch)*   a pass
*cae*   field
*capel*   chapel
*carnedd (garnedd)*, pl. *carneddau*   cairn, mountain
*carreg (garreg)*, pl. *cerrig*   rock
*carrog*   brook, torrent
*cefn (gefn)*   ridge
*celli (gelli, gelly)*   copse, grove
*ceunant*   ravine
*clogwyn*   cliff
*coch (goch)*   red
*coed*   woodland
*cors (gors)*   bog, marsh
*craig (graig)*, pl. *creigiau*   rock
*crib (grib)*, pl. *cribau*   ridge
*croes*   cross
*cwm*   valley
*cyrn (gyrn)*   peak
*dinas (din)*   fortification
*dol (ddol)*, pl. *dolydd, dolau*   meadow
*drws (ddrws)*   pass, gap, door
*du (ddu)*   black
*dulas*   dark stream
*dwr, dwfr*   water
*dwyfor*   big water
*dyffryn*   valley
*fawr*   big
*felin*   mill
*ffynnon*   spring, well
*fridd (frith)*   mountain pasture

*garth*   promontory, ridge, hill
*glan (lan)*   river bank
*glas*   green or blue
*graianog*   gravel
*gwern*   marsh
*hafod*   summer dwelling
*llwyd*   grey
*llyn*   lake
*mawr*   big
*moel*   hill, mountain
*morfa*   marsh
*mynydd*   mountain
*nant*   gorge
*newydd*   new
*pair*   cauldron
*pant*   valley, hollow
*pen (ben)*, pl. *pennau*   top, end
*penmaen*   rocky promontory
*pistyll (rhaeadr)*   spout, waterfall
*plas*   mansion
*pont (bont)*   bridge
*porth (borth)*   harbour, door, landing place
*pwll*   pool
*rhos, rhosdir*   marsh, moor, moorland
*rhyd*   ford
*sych*   dry
*tal*   end
*tan (dan)*   under, beneath
*traeth (draeth)*   shore, beach
*trwyn*   promontory
*twll*   hole
*ty*   house
*uchaf*   highest
*uwch*   above
*wen*   white
*ynys*   island, river meadow
*ystrad*   valley floor
*ystum*   bend in river

The Dark Ages were years of strife, marked by tribal warfare between the Welsh chieftains and also by Viking raids on the coastlands. It is said that Bangor Cathedral was sited hidden in its narrow valley to protect it from passing seaborne raiders. But by the 12th century the Welsh leaders had to face a different threat, this time from the Anglo-Norman armies, pushing along the North Wales coastal plain. Both Llywelyn the Great and Llywelyn ap Gruffyd fought long guerilla campaigns from their mountain strongholds of Dolbadarn Castle (Llanberis) and Dolwyddelan, while the native population were able to reoccupy the Iron Age hillforts. But eventually, the military expertise of Edward I was sufficiently powerful to overthrow the stubborn resistance and he then constructed his girdle of famous stone castles and fortified towns at all the strategic bridging points and harbours around Snowdonia. The castle towns made the first lasting impression on the landscape that you see today. Apart from the irregularly shaped Celtic fields, hillforts and Roman roads, little else of the human imprint has survived from pre-Norman times.

Notwithstanding the Glyndwr revolt of 1400, the wars of the Roses and the Civil War the next five centuries saw a gradual development of the coastal towns and villages and a slow but steady land reclamation in the central mountainland as the population grew and more food was required. Tillage was carried to heights of over 1000 feet (300 m) on the pockets of better soil in the more sheltered eastern valleys overlooking the Conwy Valley. Welsh field names above Dolgarrog suggest that even wheat was once grown on these desolate slopes, now littered with long-abandoned farmsteads. It was these hardy farmers who brought their black cattle and sheep down from the mountainland to markets in Caernarfon, Conwy and Llanrwst, or herded them along grassy drovers' roads to England. Field boundaries were pushed farther and farther up the slopes throughout the centuries and the temporary summer grazing camp ('hafod') eventually became a permanent farmhouse, albeit on poor stony soils and on exposed hillsides.

Apart from the continued clearance of the natural woodlands and the sporadic enclosure of the moorlands, Snowdonia's landscape had changed but little since the Norman invasions. It is true that there had grown up a trade in Welsh woollens, based on the mountain sheep, herbal dyes and abundance of water power at the base of the numerous waterfalls, such as those at Trefriw and in the Machno valley. Furthermore, the Wynn family of Gwydyr Castle (see Appendix) had begun to exploit the lead resources near Betws-y-Coed as early as the 16th century. But it was not until the Industrial Revolution of the 18th and 19th centuries had created an enormous demand for metal and stone that the North Welsh countryside was to suffer its greatest transformation since the Ice Age.

In the space of 100 years the mountainland was opened up. Slate and stone quarries tore holes in the hillsides to match the glacial hollows; lead, copper and zinc mines brought smoke, noise and deadly pollution to the very heart of Snowdonia, disfiguring its cwms and discolouring its lakes; most of the remaining oakwoods now disappeared into the furnaces and smelters, while the water wheels powered not only woollen mills but other types of industrial machinery. The mountains soon became criss-crossed with a network of tracks and tramways, later to be replaced with roads and railways, many of which were later to be converted for recreational rather than industrial roles. Land was reclaimed not only up the

hillsides, where extensive sheep runs were carved out of the common grazings, but also in estuaries such as the Glaslyn, where the new towns of Tremadog and Porthmadog sprang up. The engineers brought new bridges, harbours and metalled roads to the coastal towns and the tourists followed in their wake to marvel at the picturesque and sublime scenery of the newly 'discovered' uplands. But for the hill farmers and quarrymen life remained hard and the roads which brought the visitors also provided a means of escape from their bleak, rainy environment. Thus, the last few pages of the Snowdonian story book chronicle a gradual rural depopulation. The highest hill farms fell silent, the walled fields of the cwms became bracken infested. The stone and slate quarries, too, limped slowly to a halt as demand declined, leaving derelict villages and unemployed communities.

Today, the valleys are dotted with cars, caravans and camping sites, the hillsides are clothed with conifer plantations, the lake and river waters drive, not waterwheels, but electricity generators or help cool Trawsfynydd's nuclear power station. The high peaks and miners' tracks ring not to the sound of sledgehammers but to the laughter and chatter of walkers and climbers. The castles and towns are invaded by different types of people, bent on enjoyment rather than conquest. They see a landscape which is a complex mixture of physical and human threads, as tightly woven as the renowned Welsh tweeds. Each thread adds its own distinctive colour and texture to the remarkable scenery of Snowdonia.

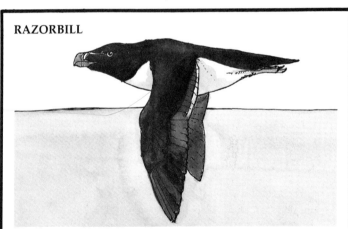

## RAZORBILL

One of Britain's common seabirds wherever there are cliffs. Jet-black and white, the razorbill is easy to distinguish if it flies close by, because of its heavy, stout, curved bill. The black and white striped bill is literally razor-sharp and is used to get a firm grip on the razorbill's fish prey. Like the guillemot (which is more brown in colour), razorbills are often among the worst hit of seabirds by oil slicks because they tend to sit in 'rafts' or groups on the sea.

(Opposite) **Natural woodlands of a mountain valley above Trefriw and an exposed hill farm (hafod) on the upper slopes**

# Mountain weather

It may be true to say that the weather is the most common topic of conversation in Britain. It becomes even more significant when you are on holiday, for it often governs the plans for the day's outing. This is particularly the case in a mountainous area for there is little apparent reward in walking in thick mist over boggy, streaming hillslopes. Yet heatwaves too, however infrequent, can bring their problems; in addition to their sizzling temperatures, which cause lassitude, the heat haze can ruin the view and therefore also most attempts at photography. Snowdonia's weather is nothing if not changeable, rarely are two consecutive days alike. It is the changing light, the cloud shadows chasing across the hills, the sunlight dancing on the ripples of the Irish Sea, the highest summits revealed for an instant by a break in the curtain of cloud – all of these add to the pleasure of a day in the hills. This chapter will attempt to explain the vagaries of mountain weather and suggest how to make the best of the conditions encountered during your visit.

First of all, you might well assimilate some facts. Snowdonia has one of the highest rainfalls in southern Britain (the average yearly precipitation on Snowdon's southern slopes is about 150 inches) and in the central mountains rain is recorded on more than 200 days per year. With all this moisture it's not surprising that there is also a great deal of cloudiness. It's worth bearing in mind that during the Ice Age the precipitation would have been in the form of snow which then became converted into ice in the cwms; it is no wonder the glaciers were so effective in carving up the landscape! Having emphasised these high rainfall figures, however, it is equally important to state that not all of Snowdonia experiences such wet conditions. In most of the coastal areas the annual rainfall is only a fraction of that in the mountainland: Llandudno, for example, receives less than 30 inches in about 130 days, while neighbouring Anglesey boasts one of the highest sunshine records in western Britain. So what leads to these curious discrepancies over such short distances?

It is all to do with the prevailing wind, the height of the hills and the degree of shelter afforded by the mountain mass (referred to as a 'rain shadow'). Most of Britain's weather comes from the Atlantic, the prevailing wind is southwesterly and since it passes across the ocean it is moisture-laden. When such a moisture-carrying wind reaches western Wales it encounters the mountain barrier of Snowdonia over which it is forced to rise. The cooling caused by the ascent to higher elevations makes the wind incapable of retaining all the moisture picked up over the ocean and it condenses as cloud. This is why clouds build up on our mountains when westerlies blow, and it is from these that rain often falls. The varying degrees of moisture, speed of wind and fall of temperature will govern not only the

(Opposite) **Hydro-electricity pipelines at Dolgarrog, leading water from mountain lakes down to a power station**

amount and the duration of the rainfall but also the height of the cloud base. Sometimes the mountains will 'wear a hat' all day, but no really heavy rain will occur, merely a misty drizzle. It is on such days (which are commonplace in Snowdonia) that many of the walks, listed below can be taken without any danger or discomfort, just so long as you have stout footwear and take an anorak or rainproof clothing in your rucksack in case of a gradual deterioration in the weather. Only Walk 2 (Snowdon summit) should be avoided in thick mist or heavy rain.

You will have realised that if much of the moisture is unloaded by westerly winds on the mountains themselves then not much will be left to fall on their eastern (leeward) slopes. Thus, the Conwy Valley and the coastal hills between Aber and Conwy are in a rain shadow and are often cloud-free. Walk 8, for example, is often remarkably dry underfoot, while Walks 1 and 5 may also be worth considering in cloudy and unsettled weather. This is equally true of Walk 7, for the western coasts of the Llyn Peninsula, although not in a rain shadow, are far enough away from the highest mountains not to be affected by the highest amounts of rainfall. This explains why Anglesey's flatness and lack of mountains is reflected in its low rainfall and high sunshine figures, even though both Anglesey and Llyn are certainly affected by the prevailing westerlies – both are on the windward side and both are notoriously windy because of the lack of shelter. Nonetheless, you may encounter some wet days, so why not make the best of them and either visit the waterfalls (especially Walks 5 and 9), brave the tumult of a storm-whipped coast (Walk 10) which can be quite a majestic experience, or simply potter around a historic town (Walk 11). A wet day may be a good opportunity to take a railway journey (the Ffestiniog Railway) or follow Drive 3 (where you can spend some time indoors).

Rain is not the only problem in deciding what to wear or where to go. Temperature is also an important concern, so it's as well to know, before setting out on your mountain walks, that temperatures usually fall about 3°F (about 1.8°C) for every 1000 feet (300 m) of ascent. Thus, you may leave the pleasant temperature of about 68°F (17°C) in your coastal resort but experience a drop of almost 10°F (or 6°C) by the time you reach the summit of a high mountain. Furthermore, exposure to wind must also be taken into account. A strengthening of the wind plus a drop in temperature, related to increasing altitude, can be a formidable combination, the effects of which are more severe than the simple sum of the two. Windchill is one of the hillwalker's greatest problems and in the most severe cases rapid loss of heat can lead to hypothermia. Thus, there are two golden rules when walking in the mountains: first, make sure that you have good footwear and waterproof clothing, and secondly, always take a woollen sweater in case of falling temperatures. You may be lucky and not need either anorak or pullover, but it's better to be safe than sorry.

While on the subject of wind, it is useful to say something about the different types of breezes that affect Snowdonia and its coast-lines. The mountain mass is large enough to generate what are termed 'valley winds' which blow in response to changing tempera-

## ROSEBAY WILLOW HERB

This is a plant that likes an open site, with a well drained soil. It will even grow well on rocky slopes. About a metre to a metre and a half tall, this stately plant carries many rosey-purple flowers about 3 cm across on its upright stem.

tures throughout the day. On warm, sunny and still mornings the air directly in contact with the mountain slopes is heated to a greater degree than air at the same level but situated vertically above the valley floor. The heated air, like that in a hot-air baloon, rises by convection and is replaced by cooler air from the valley floor. By the afternoon these up-valley breezes provide welcome relief on those rare scorching days in the mountains. At night the mechanism works in reverse, for the mountain tops then lose heat by radiation more quickly than the air in the valleys and this cools the air in contact with the upper slopes. Because cold air sinks it begins to flow down the valley as a down-valley breeze, which can be quite chilly after sunset, as visitors in Beddgelert and Betws-y-Coed have discovered. Pools of cold night air often accumulate in the high hollows, such as Cwm

Idwal, before 'overflowing' down into the valley beneath, where they bring a sudden squall of wind to unsuspecting campers. Similar unequal heating and cooling of the land and sea leads to the more common sea breezes. These are strongest in the afternoons, following hot, sunny mornings along all the North Wales' coastlines in summer. Land breezes at night are less common, except at the mouths of some of the larger valleys which channel the cooler mountain winds down to the coast.

Weather forecasts on television and in the daily press are probably too general to allow any detailed plans to be made except in periods of settled weather. But you could be your own weather forecaster by following the diagrams below.

SW                                                                    NE

Snowdon

Gentle north - easterly, easterly or south - easterly wind

Criccieth                                                          Conwy

(a) These conditions give Snowdonia its best weather conditions, with just a few fleecy 'cotton wool' clouds or some higher milky cloud; the weather will almost certainly stay fine so all of the walks or drives will be worthwhile, but remember to take a woollen sweater if you are intending to go high – try Walks 1, 2, 3 and 4

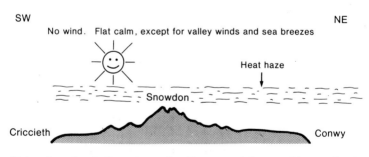

SW                                                                    NE

No wind. Flat calm, except for valley winds and sea breezes

Heat haze

Snowdon

Criccieth                                                          Conwy

(b) A prolonged spell of fine calm weather allows you to follow any of the excursions in the guide, but remember that climbing in the heat can be exhausting and the heat haze spoils photography so avoid the longest and most strenuous walks (e.g. Walks 1 and 2); the cool shade of the woodlands may seem attractive (e.g. Walks 5 and 9) but the waterfalls may not be at their best; a combination of sunny hillside and shaded valley may offer the best compromise – so try Walks 4, 6, 7 or 8

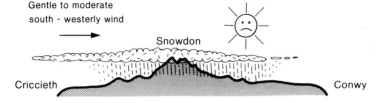

SW                                                                    NE

Gentle to moderate
south - westerly wind

Snowdon

Criccieth                                                        Conwy

(c) Uniform layer of grey cloud over windward coasts and mountains will probably
persist all day; drizzle on windward coasts and persistent rain in mountains;
possible breaks in the cloud in the NE – try Drive 1 or Walks 1, 5, 7 or 8

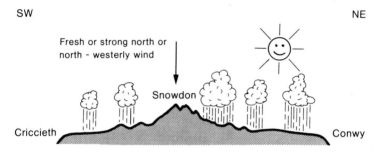

SW                                                                    NE

Fresh or strong north or
north - westerly wind

Snowdon

Criccieth                                                        Conwy

(d) Towering white shower clouds across all the region but most developed along
northern slopes; heavy showers of rain, hail or sleet and strong gusts of wind; sharp
drop of temperature in showers; excellent visibility and bright sunshine between
showers, therefore best weather for photography: but do not be fooled by the
cloud-free early morning, for by the afternoon the shower clouds will be almost
continuous – you can try almost any of the walks and drives, but not Walk 2 (note
that Walks 7 and 8 will be exposed but quite exhilarating)

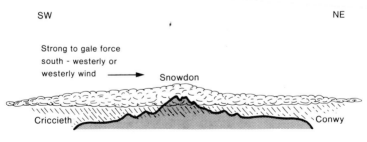

SW                                                                    NE

Strong to gale force
south - westerly or
westerly wind                         Snowdon

Criccieth                                                        Conwy

(e) Strong southwesterly winds and low cloud cover everywhere probably mean that
rain has set in for the day; the storminess and persistent downpour will be worst in
the mountains and on the windward coasts; there may be some shelter in the Conwy
Valley – you can try Walks 9, 10 and 11 or take the Ffestiniog railway journey (the
drives may not be very rewarding because your windscreen could be steamed up)

Have a nice day!

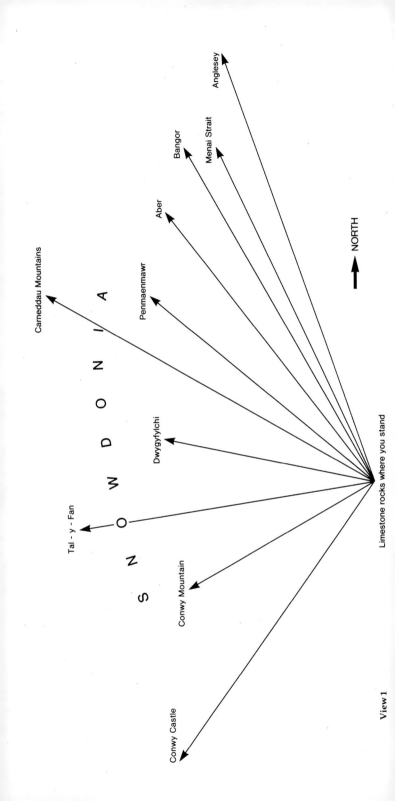

View 1

# PART 2    ROUTES

# Views: getting your bearings

## 1    From the Great Orme, Llandudno

### Introduction

From Llandudno drive [Marine Drive >] past pier entrance. Left after 1 mile (1.6km) up steep road, past church, to summit 🅿 ♿. Or take cabin lift from town centre. Llandudno 🅿 **wc M** 🅿️ 🚻 🚻 🚻 ♿ 🚻 🚻. Early closing Wednesday (except summer)

If you ignore the cable-car terminus, the tramway and the brash hotel, the summit of Llandudno's Great Orme cannot have changed too much since its early visitors, the Romans first saw the misty fastnesses of Snowdonia across the stormy waters of Conwy Bay. It still looks like Nature's obstacle course! There is a wide, tide-ripped estuary, a marshy shore, a precipitous rockbound coast and a trackless highland wilderness beyond. The massif must have appeared as impregnable then as it was to appear to Edward I and his invading English army several centuries later.

From this vantage point the rolling mountains, dodging intermittently behind passing shower clouds, may appear forbidding. Often they are silhouetted against the afternoon light or the setting winter sun, but an early riser can catch their crags lit brightly by fitful easterly sunshine. The precipitous sea cliffs of Snowdonia's north-eastern corner add to the starkness and feeling of inaccessibility. For centuries both road and rail builders have discovered this high, rocky coastline to be all but impossible to circumnavigate, finally succeeding only by remarkable feats of engineering and modern tunnelling. The same hard rocks which form the towering sea cliffs of Penmaenmawr and Penmaenbach, dreaded by early stage coach travellers, have attracted quarrymen from time immemorial. It isn't difficult to see that their slopes have been torn and pockmarked by generations of workmen who shipped away from the tiny coastal jetties millions of tons of granite to pave the cobbled streets and build the Victorian cities of England.

### The view

From the well trodden, sheep-grazed turf of the immediate foreground, with its dove-grey stone walls, rocky outcrops and unusual white stone graffiti patterned carefully on the grass, you can soon determine that the light-coloured rocks of the

Great Orme are different from those darker, harder ones of which distant Snowdonia is built. These whitish rocks are of limestone, sometimes referred to as Mountain Limestone, from which the jutting headland of the Orme has been carved. Limestone breaks down into calcium-rich, fertile soils, hence its bright-green grassland. Furthermore, lead is often associated with Mountain Limestone and was once mined here by the Romans, as in Mendip and the Peak District. On the Orme's sea cliffs the antics of a wide variety of seabirds can be enjoyed: kittiwakes, gannets, skuas, terns, guillemots, razorbills and, or course, the ubiquitous gulls. If you look left across the sea to the estuary of the river Conwy you can pick out the citadel of the walled town itself nestling strategically beneath the mountains at the bridging point (see Walk 11).

Let your eyes then travel upwards along the quarried ridge of Conwy Mountain (see Walk 8) leaving behind the neat rows of caravans on the Morfa's sandy shore. Beyond the first headland (Penmaenbach) are the woods and meadows of the sheltered 'amphitheatre' of Dwygyfylchi where an isolated patch of better soil marks some sandy boulder clay dumped by former Scottish ice sheets that had pushed a long way southwards across sandstones exposed on the Irish sea floor. Then, as now, Snowdonia's implacable coastal mountains acted as a formidable barrier. Today, the headlands of both Penmaenbach and Penmaenmawr are penetrated by road and rail tunnels to assist the modern coastal traveller. Penmaenmawr's gaunt headland has been terribly disfigured by quarrying, with only a lonely pimple now surviving to show its former natural summit. Even the Stone Age axe factory has been destroyed.

Beyond the scarred bastion, however, broad expanses of smooth coastal farmland reappear, stretching past Llanfairfechan and Aber (see Walk 9) all the way to Bangor and the Menai Strait. Like the Dwygyfylchi lowland these coastal fields, with their trim hedgerows, owe their existence to the thick layer of relatively fertile red, sandy, coastal boulder clay heaped up by the same northern glaciers against the dark, rocky flanks of Snowdonia's north-facing slopes. Such soil fertility is rare in the true mountainland for, by and large, the local Welsh soils are sour, heavy, wet and stony, incapable of supporting much more than poor scrub and rough grazing unless carefully managed.

Away to the right of the Menai Strait lies the

fertile isle of Anglesey, once the Welsh granary both for Romans and for Edward's invading English army. You will not be surprised to learn that the plains, rolling hills, well drained sandy soils, nutritious limestone rocks, low elevation and high sunshine hours have combined to give to Anglesey a distinct farming advantage over neighbouring Snowdonia. But the mountainland has other advantages, which you will discover when you venture into the interior. Its rugged scenic grandeur, its crags, lakes, waterfalls, sylvan glades, mysterious misty hollows, and its ever-changing light. Such is the stuff from which romantic legends are made and which contributes to the pleasures of the tourist who seeks both the awesome and the picturesque. On clear days, if you look beyond the outer ramparts of the coastal hills you will see some of the mightiest peaks of the Carneddau, with the highest (Carnedd Llywelyn) named after the most famous of Welsh medieval princes. It may have been from a spot similar to that where you are now standing that Edward I's generals stood, pondering their strategy, planning their castle building and wondering how to defeat this great Welsh medieval chieftain in his mountain stronghold. Perhaps they too marvelled at the scenic prospect?

## 2  From near Menai Bridge

*Introduction*

From Menai Bridge town follow A4080 (previously A5) [Holyhead >] for almost 1 mile (1km). **P** in lay-by on main road. Menai Bridge **P wc M** [PO] ⊘ 🛈 ♿ ♨ ➦

No other of North Wales' vantage points gives such a vivid impression of Snowdonia's grandeur than that from the Anglesey shore of the Menai Strait. The long curving sweep of the mountainous skyline southwestwards from Conwy's breezy estuary to Yr Eifl's iron-bound sea cliffs creates one of Britain's finest panoramas, especially when springtime snows crown the summits. The seemingly impregnable mountain wall, rising abruptly from the coastal plain, is breached only sporadically by deeply etched passes into which the routeways burrow furtively, as if venturing into a gigantic fortress. From Anglesey, these mountains probably looked just as unyielding to Edward I's invading troops some 700 years ago. No network of roads, hedges, walls and pylons would have greeted their eyes, it is true, but the rocky crags and heathery slopes have hardly changed at all over the intervening centuries. But not so on the skirting coastal plain for here modern

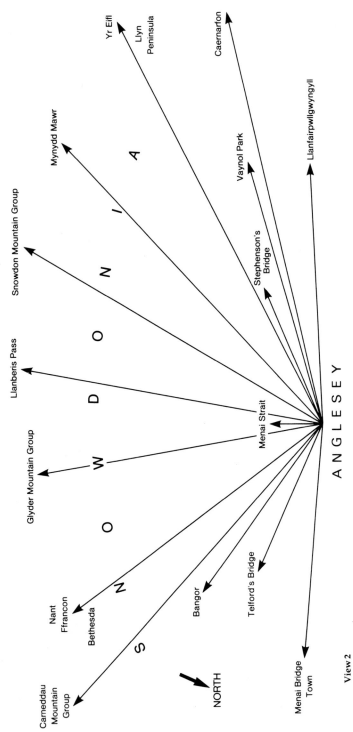

View 2

society has left its indelible imprint. Bustling towns, factories, pylons, roads and bridges, cars, trains, boats, all crowd into your view, bringing a sense of reassurance because of their familiarity. Beyond lies the mysterious wilderness, tempting you to unlock its fascinating portals and explore its inner recesses, especially when sunshine and cloud shadows dapple the summits and pick out the wrinkles in Snowdonia's gnarled countenance.

## The view

For those of you who have already driven through Snowdonia's passes and gazed up at its soaring precipices and jagged peaks, the view from Anglesey may come as a surprise, for the general impression of the mountainland is now one of a gently curving dome. The ruggedness of the interior is not apparent from afar and all the mountains appear to be flat topped. This is because the viewpoint has changed and the detailed irregularities have merged into the background of the broad mountain flanks, when seen from a distance. Only the smooth outlines of rolling mountains cut by deep valleys can be discerned. It took many millions of years for the earliest rivers to cut their valleys into Snowdonia's gently domed surface, but then the Ice Age glaciers, within a few thousand years, quickly broke down the defences of the mountain fortress as they poured in force along the valleys and through the breaches, creating the passes which you will later explore. The crags and pinnacles can be likened, therefore, to the raw and broken edges of the breached defences, but above and beyond them the towers and turrets of Snowdonia's fortress remain virtually intact, scarred and sullied perhaps, but as yet relatively unbroken by nature's attacking forces.

The two biggest breaches can be seen ahead, to the left the Nant Ffrancon, to the right the Llanberis pass. Although not quite visible from this viewpoint, at each of these portals a town has grown up, not as you might expect to guard the passes but in response to the value of the underlying rocks. The northern bastions of the mountains themselves have been built from slaty rocks which, paradoxically, while not resisting the bludgeoning attacks of the glaciers are able, having been split mechanically into thin slices, to withstand the vagaries of British weather when used as roofing slates. Thus the towns of Bethesda and Llanberis grew rapidly around their quarries in response to the urban demands of the Industrial Revolution, only to wane as 20th century clay tiles gradually replaced these natural rock slivers as roofing materials, because of the cheaper production costs.

The Industrial Revolution created many inventors and designers, two of whom, Thomas Telford and Robert Stephenson, made major contributions to the scene now spread before you. Try to imagine the problems once faced by travellers when confronted by the tide-ripped waters of the Menai Strait. Journeys to Anglesey and thence to Ireland were fraught with danger until these eminent bridge builders came along. The graceful road bridge to your left, with its central span of 579 feet (176 m), became, in 1820, the world's first large iron suspension bridge. Its 16 massive suspension chains disappear 60 feet (18 m) back into the rock in tunnels blasted by Telford's engineers. Until very recently this was the only road bridge over the fearsome strait and it was the last link in Telford's London to Holyhead road on which you are now standing. To your right, Stephenson's Britannia railway bridge was started in 1846 and originally comprised twin metal tubes supported on three gigantic stone towers. After a major fire had seriously damaged it in 1970 a second road bridge was constructed above the refurbished railway track, its span now strengthened by an arch of steel girders. Alongside it stride the pylons carrying electricity from Anglesey's nuclear power station to join the national grid, now boosted by Dinorwig's hydro-electric power generated in Llanberis's defunct slate quarries (see Drive 2).

Human ingenuity has finally overcome the natural obstacle of the Menai Strait which had defied the efforts of man for centuries. But although it is a substantial, sea-filled channel, the Menai Strait is a very recent feature, geologically speaking. It certainly pales into insignificance when both its age and its stature are compared, for example, with the Straits of Dover. From many viewpoints it looks more like a river and in some ways that's what it once was, or rather two rivers, one flowing northeastwards the other southwestwards. Until the closing phases of the Ice Age the spot where you are now standing was a divide between the two, but some 20 000 years ago melting waters, trapped beneath a thick ice sheet, tore out a narrow rocky gorge in the vicinity of the present Telford bridge. After the ice had disappeared the gorge (like that now followed by the A4087 road from

Port Dinorwig into Bangor) stood high and dry – completely streamless. But as the water once locked-up in the world's ice sheets returned to the oceans the sea level slowly rose, flooding the two short river valleys in question. Finally it flooded the linking gorge and completed the strait which you see today, thus making Anglesey into an island for the first time. That is why the landscapes on either side of the Menai Strait look so similar; both were once part of the same coastal plain. Ice sheets also blanketed the hard rocks of the plain with thick layers of glacial debris, composed largely of clays, sands and gravels. Where this cover occurs quite prosperous farms flourish on its fertile soils. On the intervening rocky ridges and on the neighbouring foothills, however, the glacial mantle is thin or absent. Thus, their soils are sour and poorly developed. Gorse, bracken and scrubby thickets replace the farmlands on these less favoured sites, so the distant hill farms that you can see are often battling to make ends meet in their more hostile environment. Not surprisingly, therefore, more and more sheep farms are being given over to forestry, thus creating slopes now patched with dark-green blocks of conifer woodland. Their geometric outlines and sombre colouring contrast with the sporadic splashes of frothy green oakwoods which clothe both the nearby shorelines and the demesnes of the neighbouring stately homes.

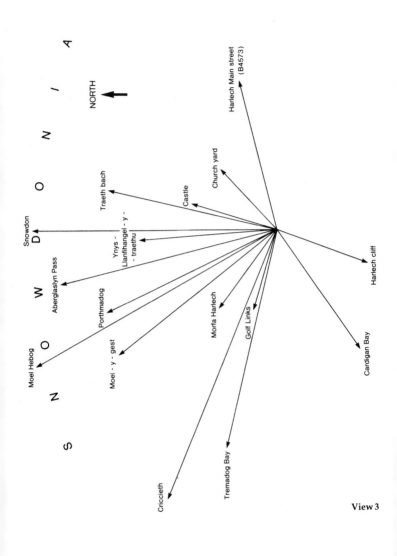

S
N
O
W
D
O
N
I
A

NORTH

Snowdon

Traeth bach

Castle

Church yard

Harlech Main street
(B4573)

Ynys -
Llanfihangel - y -
- traethu

Aberglaslyn Pass

Porthmadog

Moel Hebog

Moel - y - gest

Morfa Harlech

Golf Links

Harlech cliff

Cardigan Bay

Criccieth

Tremadog Bay

View 3

# 3   From Harlech

## Introduction

From 🅿 on main street follow B4573 south for 400 yards (400 m) to rocky knoll on right. Harlech 🅿 WC 🅿 Ø 👜 🚻 ♿ 🍴 ♥. Castle opening times in Appendix

This is unquestionably one of Wales' most famous views, partly because it encompasses a superb stretch of sandy coastline, partly for its dramatic foreground of Harlech Castle on its windy crag, but mainly because on a clear day you can see Snowdon in its conical splendour. It is a vista quite different from the others because, from here, the mountainland appears to be more rugged and dissected. Furthermore, around noon the sun is at your back so that instead of stark silhouettes, each hillside and summit is etched in clear detail. You can admire the view from the castle itself or better still, if you want a dramatic photograph (to include this wonderful fortress) walk a few hundred yards southwards along the town's main street to a small rocky headland.

## The view

The rugged grandeur of the northern skyline forms a perfect backdrop to the scene. Due north the lumpy mass of Moel Hebog is terminated abruptly eastwards by the abyss of the Aberglaslyn Pass beyond which the stately pyramid of Snowdon forms the culminating peak. To its right the sharp-ridged Cnicht and the hump-backed Moelwyns, above the Vale of Ffestiniog, complete the frame of uplands, all deeply scarred and chiselled by the glaciers of the Ice Age.

Imagine this scene some 20 000 years ago when broad tongues of ice emerged from the Glaslyn gorge and the Vale of Ffestiniog before coalescing into an enormous lobe of ice which stretched far out into Tremadog Bay. It would have been like a landscape on the fringes of modern Antarctica. Because much of the Earth's moisture was locked up in ice sheets the sea level would have been much lower, so that the open ocean would have been invisible from here; it had retreated 50 miles or more to the west. At the end of the Ice Age, as the water returned to the oceans, the Irish Sea would have set about encroaching rapidly back into view as its level quickly rose again. It first attacked the flat plain of glacial debris dumped by the glaciers and found it no great obstacle. Catastrophic coastal floods would have become common place, leading to the legends of lost cities and submerged kingdoms along this coastline. But this was long before man had settled in Britain so that the lines of submerged stones beneath Cardigan Bay (e.g. *Sarn Badrig* = St Patrick's Causeway) are not city streets or buildings but merely groups of massive glacial boulders marking the limits of the ice sheets: today we call them submerged 'moraines'. As the coastline was driven landwards it finally reached the line of hard gritstone, where Harlech now stands, and here its progress was halted some 5000 years ago. But, just to the north, the sea gradually flooded the ice-deepened estuaries of Traeth Mawr and Traeth Bach until its waters lapped the foot of the Aberglaslyn Pass itself (see Walk 6). The small rocky foothills were then converted into islands, including the broad hump of Ynys Llanfihangel-y-traethu which rises abruptly from the marsh at the northern end of Morfa Harlech. It is interesting that its highest point is termed Ogof Foel (the bare hill of the cave), suggesting that the waves once carved out weaknesses in this low rocky eminence. A smaller 'island', Lasynys, can be seen nearer to the right, if you are viewing from the castle.

Today, the coastline has changed again, for in places the land has gained upon the sea, incorporating some of the former islands, while in the early 19th century Mr. Madocks reclaimed most of the Glaslyn estuary by building his embankment and the new town of Porthmadog (Drives 2 and 3) which peeps out from behind Ynys Llanfihangel. But the most dramatic change has been the gradual growth of the marsh and dune complex which fills the foreground, now known as Morfa Harlech.

When Harlech Castle was constructed in 1286 it possessed a watergate, and several 14th-century documents refer to Harlech as a port. The former sea cliff on which the fortress stands is now far from the sea, so what has happened? If you were able to examine the modern sea cliffs one mile (1.6 km) south of the castle you would see that they are formed of glacial boulder clay. Until the building of the railway embankment, which acted as a defence, these cliffs would have been under savage wave attack for centuries, the fallen material being carried northwards by waves and currents, pushed by the prevailing southwesterly winds. Eventually a narrow finger of shingle and sand would have extended from the old Harlech Cliff out into Tremadog Bay. As this grew northwards, sand dunes began to develop along it and tidal marshes grew behind it. The beach ridge would have formed a sheltered harbour at Harlech on a notoriously stormy coast. Thus, King Edward, seeing possibilities of supplying his rocky fortress from the sea, sited his castle above this shallow anchorage. In the succeeding centuries the beach ridge grew longer, the marshes broader and the creeks shallower so that tides no longer reached the watergate. In 1808 an embankment was built eastwards from Ynys Llanfihangel, finally closing off most of the tidal creeks from the Traeth Bach estuary. Long before then the military function of Harlech Castle had ceased and the port had declined by the 15th century. Today Morfa Harlech, having been drained, is a mosaic of dunes, grazing lands, golf links and caravan parks. A housing estate and sports centre flourish where ships once anchored, a conifer plantation now blankets the marsh in the middle distance. It's hard to believe that 13th-century soldiers on the castle's battlements would have seen virtually unbroken sea water stretching between Harlech and the Aberglaslyn Pass. Not a car or tourist would have been in sight!

# SCOTS PINE

(100–160 ft; 30–50 m)

The tree of upland heath, lowland sand and dry rocky mountain sides, the Scots pine demands few nutrients from the soil on which it grows. Its main requirement is a well drained site. In common with all pines, the needles are borne on the twigs in groups of two, three or five. Scots pine cones are characteristically nobbly with pointed scales. The most easily distinguished features of the tree are the absence of low, level branches, its orange to red–brown flaking bark and its layered leaves confined to the crown space.

(Opposite) **Harlech Castle on its gritstone cliff**

# Drives in and around Snowdonia

## 1   The eastern plateaux and the Conwy Valley
Conwy–Betws-y-Coed–Trefriw–Conwy

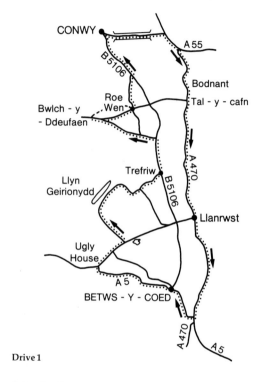

**Drive 1**

*Introduction*
The countryside which lies along the eastern flanks
of Snowdonia is altogether gentler than that of the
central mountainland. It is lower in elevation, less
rugged, more pastoral and considerably more
forested. This is due, in no small measure, to the
presence of Snowdonia's longest river, the Conwy,
which gathers together all the east-flowing streams
and carries them bodily northwards to the sea. The
Conwy's remarkable flat-floored vale (no less than
14 miles (22 km) in length between Betws-y-Coed
and the estuary) extends a long arm of lowland
deep into the eastern plateaux. Thus, your drive is,
in the main, one of easy gradients along the
comfortable valley floor, but to add some zest the
route occasionally leaps suddenly into the wilder-

ness. Twice you will leave the main road and follow narrow, twisting lanes that will take you high into the lonely hidden valleys of the mountain fastness. Many of these lanes are single track, so beware oncoming traffic and walkers! Some of the gradients are extremely steep so make certain that your brakes are good and that you engage low gears when necessary. The views which unfold make the detours worthwhile and there are plenty of picnic spots. The route is about 37 miles (59 km) long, a dozen of which are on narrow by-roads, so allow at least half a day. The drive starts from the historic town of Conwy.

Conwy 🅿 wc 🅿 Ø
🏛 M 🚻 ⌂ 🛗 ♨.
Walk 11. Early
closing Wednesday.
Castle opening times
in Appendix

### The route

From Conwy east on
A55 through
Llandudno Junction.
Follow A470
[Betws-y-Coed >]

After crossing the Conwy river eastwards to Llandudno Junction look back at the historic grey stone fortress crouched at the feet of the mountains (see Walk 11), where it commands both the coastal and the valley routeways. The red rash of ribbon-built housing and the new estates of Glan Conwy are soon left behind as you leave the riverside to climb over the first of the wooded hills. Here, to the left, are the splendours of Bodnant Gardens, famed not only for their magnificent trees, shrubs and flowers, but also for the splendid views of Snowdonia which their sculptured terraces afford.

Bodnant Gardens
(NT). See Appendix

Tal-y-cafn 🛗 Ø

At Tal-y-cafn the valley narrows as the river crosses hard beds of rock which also provide firm footings for another bridge. On the far bank the Ferry Hotel reminds you that this was once the easiest crossing place of the long marshy valley. The Romans were quick to discover this and built their fort at Canovium on the west bank to guard both the ferry and their mountain road westwards to Segontium (Caernarfon). Later in your journey you will follow part of that very road.

The modern valley road hugs the eastern flank of the vale all the way to Llanrwst and if you look at the marshy riverine meadows on your right you can see why. There are no roads or houses out in those green waterlogged fields and the railway runs high on an embankment above the Conwy's flood plain. Often the river spills over from its channel, turning the centre of the vale into a lake.

Llanrwst 🅿 wc 🅿 Ø
🏛 ⌂ 🛗 ♨ M
(Forestry
Commission). Early
closing Thursday.
For Gwydyr Castle
see Appendix

Even the fringes of the old town of Llanrwst are inundated on occasion, but not its ancient church and market square which perch high and dry on a mound of gravel just above the flood level. Standing midway in the vale, Llanrwst was once a place where mountain farmers came to sell their black cattle and to buy the goods brought by itinerant English traders. For centuries it was one of the last trading posts on the fringes of the wild mountain-land. Beyond its narrow hump-backed bridge lay trackless, rugged wastes, mist-shrouded and rain-lashed, whose scenic grandeur remained undis-covered by tourists until the 19th century.

Betws-y-Coed **P** **wc**
**PO** ∅ **M** **I** 🏠 🔌 💧.
Walk 5. Early closing
Thursday

It was the influx of daring Victorian visitors, venturing into North Wales along the newly built Holyhead Road (the modern A5), which led to the sudden mushrooming of Betws-y-Coed (the 'small church in the wood'). As you cross the splendid Waterloo bridge and turn westwards along the cleverly engineered A5 road, spare a thought for Thomas Telford, that colossus of the Industrial Revolution, without whose genius you would never have been able to drive in such comfort through Snowdonia. His suspension bridges, like the one at Conwy, are deservedly historic monu-ments. Betws is certainly 'in the wood', sur-rounded by quiet forested hillsides, but usually busy with traffic (mainly cars but occasionally trains) and pulsating with tourists. It has the vibrancy of a frontier town where walkers 'take to the hills' or strollers seek out the picturesque river gorges (see Walk 5).

Here, you must temporarily relinquish the easy gradients of the lowland corridor and turn west into the tributary Llugwy valley. Shortly, you may wish to stretch your legs by visiting the fabled Swallow Falls where the river appears to explode into several streams before descending as a foam-ing white deluge into a narrow gorge, carved from dark slaty rocks.

Swallow Falls
**P** **wc** ∅ 🔌 💧

After crossing river
turn sharp right on
to by-road at Ugly
House

A mile (1.6 km) upstream, where the main road crosses the river, is Ty-hyll ('ugly house') a 15th-century dwelling fashioned from enormous blocks of volcanic rock, as if by an irresponsible ogre. Its roughly textured character contrasts with the smoothly worn slate steps of its garden entrance, as if to demonstrate at a human scale the differences in rock formation which lie in the forests ahead.

The side road climbs steeply up into the wooded hills, creeping first beneath frowning cliffs of volcanic rock before emerging, after one mile (1.6 km), at a picnic site, laid out at a splendid viewpoint. It's worth pausing here awhile to look at the vista. The forested uplands stretch away to the south, one flat-topped ridge succeeding another. Apart from the intervening valleys the plateaux present a smooth tableland because the

❄ **P**

*Drives* 44

**Betws-y-Coed's large Victorian church reflects its 19th-century growth as a resort**

rocks which build them lie in horizontal or gently tilted layers. Furthermore, these shaly and slaty rocks are so similar in character that they have worn down uniformly. In the forested hills which lie behind you, however, the slates and mudstones alternate with more resistant volcanic rocks, giving a sharply stepped appearance to the scene. Remember that many of the Snowdonian volcanoes, about 500 million years ago, erupted periodically on the sea floor, so that their lavas, ash layers and beds of other ejected material became sandwiched between layers of ocean mud or sand. Because the harder volcanics have resisted nature's assault more successfully they now project their bony ribs as lines of cliffs through their forest raiment.

*Eastern plateaux and Conwy Valley* 45

**Ty-hyll ('ugly house'), a rustic dwelling built in 1475**

During a later episode of Earth history all these rock layers were themselves heaved and split by crustal turmoil. Earthquakes tore them asunder along deep fractures, and molten lava, accompanied by hot chemical solutions, again invaded from below. This witches brew permeated the cracks where it cooled to create the veins of quartz which you sometimes see lacing the rocks like dribbles of white paint. More importantly, the alchemy had also charged the veins with rich metallic deposits of lead, zinc, copper and gold. Although in the next few miles you will pass into lead- and zinc-mining country, do not expect to see the Yukon, for mining has now ceased (although one of the mines was hopefully called the Klondyke). Now almost all the buildings are derelict, the waste tips overgrown. But in the scarred landscape one of the old mines has been cleverly converted to an adventure school. A word of warning – mine shafts litter the forest, so don't venture off the beaten track! The usual tourist route carries on downhill back to the Conwy valley at Gwydyr Castle, but your route turns left to explore the lonely valley in which Llyn Geirionydd lies. As you drive through the Gwydyr Forest, first planted by the Forestry Commission in 1921, have you noticed that not all the conifer trees are the same? To most untrained eyes they may be indistinguishable, but the forester has an eye for country. By a system of trial and error he discovered; that the Snowdonian climate was too wet for European larch but suitable for Japanese larch; that Sitka spruce was better on high ground and Norwegian spruce on lower, poorly drained areas; that Lodgepole pine flourished on the rocky, more exposed patches.

Turn left (unsignposted) just before small lake on right

Llyn Geirionydd 🅿. Picnic site

Last century the waters of Llyn Geirionydd were artificially raised to provide power for the now defunct ore-crushing mills. Today, sail boats and kayaks skim their surface and an attractive picnic site adorns their southern shores. The woods at the lake's northern end, however, are slashed with a derelict mine-working to remind you of its industrial past. In fact it is a dead lake, devoid of fish and water plants, because of the high lead content of its waters which have drained across veins of lead in the catchment area.

Bear left in Llanrhychwyn 🅾 [Trefriw >] (*not* Llanrwst)

Before descending steeply into the vale of Conwy there is a remarkable glimpse of Trefriw through the valley-side woods. It sits snugly on the lower slopes astride the brawling stream of the Afon Crafnant which finally reaches the valley floor in a flurry of white water. The steepened gradient of this side valley as it meets the vale is due to overdeepening by the main Conwy valley glacier some 20 000 years ago, as it ploughed its way northwards. The tributary valleys then carried smaller streams of ice which were less successful in lowering their own floors. When all the ice had melted, the depth of the main trough was such that the side valleys were left 'hanging' at a higher elevation, and today their juvenile streams fall steeply in falls and cataracts as they race to join the mature Conwy river. As their tumbling waters

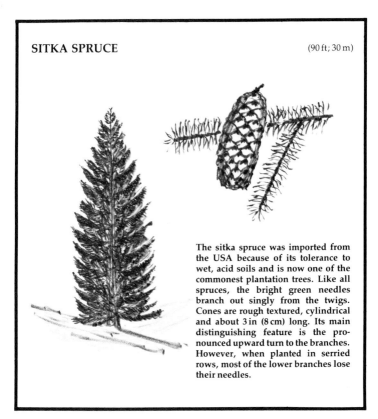

## SITKA SPRUCE

(90 ft; 30 m)

The sitka spruce was imported from the USA because of its tolerance to wet, acid soils and is now one of the commonest plantation trees. Like all spruces, the bright green needles branch out singly from the twigs. Cones are rough textured, cylindrical and about 3 in (8 cm) long. Its main distinguishing feature is the pronounced upward turn to the branches. However, when planted in serried rows, most of the lower branches lose their needles.

reach the valley floor, they jettison their muddy and rocky burden as a sloping fan-shaped apron. You will see similar fans at intervals along the trunk valley of the Conwy, wherever a mountain stream debouches on to its floor. They are especially prominent at either end of the village of Dolgarrog (see Walk 1). Not only do fans provide settlement sites, safely above the valley floods, but the steep stream gradient also offers constant water power. Not surprisingly, the combination of cheap power, mountain sheep, soft water and local vegetable dyes has led to the establishment of a Welsh woollen industry in hamlets like Trefriw. A visit to its thriving mill will be both rewarding and instructive.

Trefriw ☐ wc ⊘ ☎ ⏚ ☕. For woollen mill see Appendix. Turn left on B5106 [Conwy >]

The drive north to Dolgarrog affords excellent views of the river Conwy and its artificial embankments, termed 'dykes' (or 'levees'). These were

(Opposite) **Trefriw, sited where a tributary stream reaches the Conwy Valley floor**

constructed to control its seasonal floods but have met with no great success. This is partly because the river is tidal to Trefriw, so that high tides occasionally block the escape of excess river discharge after periods of heavy rainfall. This heavy mountain rainfall has some benefits, however, for almost the entire drainage of eastern Snowdonia has been incorporated into a complicated network of lakes and reservoirs linked by tunnels and artificial channels termed 'leats'. The combined flow is led finally into two massive pipes which plunge down the hillside at Dolgarrog. Here it drives the turbines of an electricity generating station. In turn the presence of abundant electricity accounts for the location of the aluminium works. Today, ore is no longer imported, but has been replaced by aluminium ingots brought from abroad (see Walk 1).

Dolgarrog 𝒞 ⌂.
Walk 1

The original settlement of Porth-llwyd, astride the Porth-llwyd stream, was the scene of a frightful disaster in 1925 (see Walk 1) when torrential rains caused the collapse of the dam on a mountain reservoir. The sudden release of 3 million cubic metres of water tore enormous 500 tonne boulders from the upland valley floor, and carried them to the lip of the Dolgarrog waterfall from whence they rained down on the unsuspecting village. The church and dozens of houses were inextricably buried and many people died. If you stop at the bridge the pile of boulders can still be seen despite the subsequent tree growth. When you think that at its height the flood was 27 times greater than the peak flow of the Thames in London you can grasp the enormity of this tragic event.

Turn left at Y-Bedol
inn [Llanbedr-y-
cennin >]

The final detour into the mountainland takes you first through Llanbedr-y-cennin before zigzagging beneath the power lines up the valley of the Afon Roe. After climbing steadily across featureless moorland for some three miles (4.8 km) you will finally join a Roman road at 1250 feet (380 m) above sea level. Although you can drive along it for less than a mile (< 1.6 km) you may feel like a walk to the highest part (1375 ft, 420 m) of the pass (Bwlch-y-Ddeufaen) where you can see the two prehistoric standing stones which give the pass its name ('pass of the two stones'). It also affords a glimpse of Anglesey and the northern coast but it is a windy, lonely place. As you hurry back to your car you might spare a thought for the plight of the Roman soldiers, far from their sunny homeland, struggling to build this aerial highway in the swirling mists. Today, in place of their legions, lines of pylons march stiffly through the pass.

Return on same road for 1 mile (1.6 km), turn left to Roe Wen
**P** **wc** 𝄞 🅿 🍴.
Rejoin B5106
[Conwy >]

Your route now returns to the Afon Roe and you descend rapidly along its northern bank to the pretty village of Roe Wen, famous for its tea rooms. From here it is merely a short drive through undulating, attractive farming country back to your starting point at Conwy.

At any time during the last few miles of the drive you will note the contrast between the rough moorlands you have left behind and the more fertile farmlands of these low foothills. It is largely a matter of different rock types producing contrasting slopes and soils. To the west the more rugged scenery, the stonier, thinner and more acid soils occur on the harder volcanic rocks, which are of no great value for farming. To the east of a line drawn from Conwy through Trefriw to Betws-y-Coed the rocks are 100 million years younger and produce gentler slopes because they are generally less resistant. Their soils are thicker, less stony and have more nutrients, hence the orderly farming scene. The junction of the two rock types follows an enormous vertical crack in the Earth's crust, known to geologists as the Conwy Valley Fault, caused by primeval convulsions. Rivers and glaciers have picked away at this line of weakness over millions of years, finally producing the long narrow corridor of the Vale of Conwy, its rocky floor now buried beneath some 400 feet (120 m) of glacial rubbish and modern river muds.

# 2   The central mountains and western valleys
## Caernarfon–Pen-y-Pass–Beddgelert–Tremadog– Rhyd Ddu–Caernarfon

*Introduction*
Not surprisingly, the highest mountain of Snowdonia attracts a large proportion of North Wales' walkers, but this drive allows a circumnavigation of the shapely peak to be made without leaving your car. Additionally, it lures you off the beaten track into some interesting western valleys and takes you to the starting points of two half-day mountain walks (Walks 4 and 6). The drive offers a great variety of landscapes and many opportunities to picnic. It crosses the main Welsh slate belt with its gargantuan man-made hollows, it climbs through the stark grandeur of Snowdonia's highest

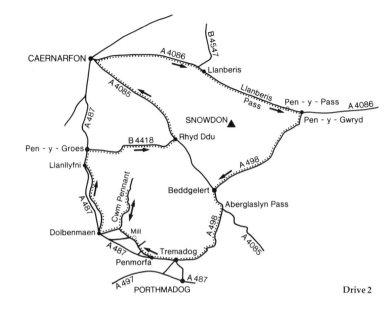

Drive 2

pass before delving into the recesses of the less-frequented western fringes. Here are quiet pastoral valleys, scattered hill farms and extensive tracts of woodland scenery, all backed by tempting glimpses of the sea. The first half of the journey follows main roads. The return journey, however, makes use of narrow byways where you can dawdle a little or stop for a leisurely picnic. It is possible to complete the drive in half a day, but with so much to see and the occasional stroll to enjoy it is better to make it into a rewarding day out. The drive starts at Caernarfon and the distance is about 62 miles (100 km).

Caernarfon 🅿 **wc** ℹ
**M** ⊘ 🏛 PO ☕ 🍴 ♿.
Early closing
Thursday. For castle
and Segontium see
Appendix

### The route

From Caernarfon
take A4086
[Llanberis >]

The main road from Caernarfon leads you quickly across the coastal hillocks and past the straggling foothill village of Llanrug until it brings you finally to the portals of the true mountainland at Cwm-y-glo. To savour the scenic splendour in full (and perhaps pause to take a photograph from this well known viewpoint) turn left off the main road and stop near the old bridge facing the majestic stretch of water known as Llyn Padarn. If you are fortunate enough to find the peaks cloud free you can pick out the summit of Snowdon to the right of the pass, looking disconcertingly insignificant as it peeps over the jostling shoulders of its satellites. But be

⚶ Park on lay-by
(B4547) and walk to
old road bridge

*Drives* 52

patient, later in the journey you will see it soar as majestically as the long-departed eagles which some believe gave Snowdon its Celtic name Eryri.

Your attention is drawn inexorably along the silvery waters of the lake and up into the dark, somewhat forbidding chasm of the Llanberis Pass, for this is the direction which you are soon to follow. But first look around at the legacy of nature's glacial handiwork. Nearby, those lakeside bluffs, straddled with scattered pines, have a story to tell. From where you stand the rocks look angular and broken, but if you were to venture to their up-valley side they would appear rounded and compact, smoothly polished as if they had been sandpapered. And, in a sense, that is what has happened, for the thick valley glacier which once pushed relentlessly down the pass carried a bouldery burden which chiselled, rasped and planed away at the bedrock until it was worn down to the present level. In the hard volcanics and gritstones of the far skyline the glacier's eroding powers were narrowly confined, as if in the jaws of a vice, but once it reached the less resistant Llanberis slate belt its tools (boulders) were able to gouge both deeper and wider to create a linear trench, later to be flooded by lake waters. One final barrier of extremely obdurate primeval rock stood in its way before the glacier was allowed to surge out onto the lowlands. This ridge of tough rock flanking your viewpoint forced the ice to grind upwards over its ramp, scraping and scouring the upslope side but wrenching and plucking away great chunks of bedrock on the ultimate downslope to produce its rugged, fractured character.

Llanberis 🅿 **wc** 🏤
∅ 🛈 ☞ 🛗 ♨ **M**.
Early closing Wednesday. For Dinorwig Power Station see Appendix

If you now return to the car and continue you will soon pass through the mountain resort of Llanberis, thronged with tourists, as it has been since Victorian times. The modern road now hugs the lakeside using the former track of the old LMS (London Midland & Scottish) railway which once sent a branch line here. When visitors had switched to cars, however, its demise was inevitable, although Llanberis itself continues to flourish as a tourist centre.

Away to your left is the Llanberis Lake Railway (see Appendix), a converted slate quarry line which now carries passengers along the farther shore of the lake from the Gilfach Ddu station in the Llyn Padarn Country Park. You cannot fail to have heard of the other famous train which starts from Llanberis, the Snowdon Mountain Railway, but that experience can be reserved for another day (see Appendix).

Llanberis is sited where a large mountain stream tumbles down into the valley. Over the centuries this torrent has carried so much debris from Snowdon's northern cwms that it has built out a large delta into the valley lake which accumulated here after the ice had disappeared. Thus, what was once a 3½ mile (5.6 km) lake has now been converted into two; Llyn Padarn and Llyn Peris.

As you look across the narrow isthmus dividing the lakes you cannot fail but to be impressed by the gigantic slate quarry which scars the mountainside. This is Dinorwig, one of the 'big three' Welsh slate quarries (Penrhyn quarry at Bethesda and the Blaenau Ffestiniog quarries are the others) which, until the 1960s, were the main source of industrial employment in Snowdonia. Entire communities depended on the extraction of slate which was once exported to all corners of the British Isles. Virtually all quarrying has now ceased here, as modern roofing materials, high finishing costs and rising transport rates have all but killed the famous Welsh slate industry. Look at its legacy; the purple, green and grey rock faces of its galleries and the seemingly endless piles of waste. But at Dinorwig not all is forlorn, for an ingenious hydroelectric scheme has been installed in the abandoned quarry by remarkable engineering feats (see Appendix). It's a fascinating story, and may repay a visit on a separate occasion, but the workings of a similar scheme have been described elsewhere (see Drive 3). Before leaving Lyn Peris it's worth noting that because its waters are an integral part of the new hydroelectric scheme the lake had to be drained and its fish (including the rare char) permanently transferred to a high-level cwm lake in eastern Snowdonia (Ffynnon Llugwy).

The southeastern end of the quarries marks the point where the older, slaty rocks give way to the tougher grits and volcanic rocks of the central mountainland. From here the valley walls close in, the mountains soar ever higher, the crags threaten, the road steepens, the car engine labours – you are at last in the very heart of the North Welsh fortress.

There are few opportunities for parking in the pass itself but during the ascent you will be driving slowly enough to pick out the main features of this narrow defile. Because of the twisting road and restricted parking it is difficult to stop to take photographs except at the small car park about half

Small 🅿 about 2½ miles (4 km) above Lyn Peris. Parking prohibited elsewhere in pass

**Giant Gromlech boulders in the Llanberis Pass**

way up. The cliffs on the left include the sheer climbing face of Dinas Gromlech which rises from the hillside like a gigantic cenotaph. The enormous boulders grouped near the road have clearly fallen from this cliff, splintered away by former frost-shattering. On the right-hand side of the pass is a fine example of a cliff produced when one of Snowdon's major ridges was drastically sliced off by the glacier in the valley. This cliff is Dinas Mot whose steepness is emphasised because its

*Central mountains and western valleys* 55

precipice is carved from a thick layer of very hard volcanic rock known as 'dolerite', which was squeezed laterally as a subterranean stream of molten lava between the existing rock layers many millions of years ago. It now stands like a tough slice of meat in a sandwich. Finally, near the head of the pass, look up to the skyline and you will see occasional boulders teetering at the brink of the valley sides, dumped in these precarious locations by the glacier. Thus they do not belong to the solid rock upon which they perch, nor have they fallen from the slopes above (like the Gromlech boulders already noted) but instead have been transported by ice, possibly for several miles from their original source further south.

Pen-y-Pass 🅿.
Walk 2
Pen-y-Gwryd 🅿 🍴.
Turn right on A498
[Beddgelert >]

Your pace now quickens as the gradient eases off at Pen-y-Pass, and after turning south at the well known hotel of Pen-y-Gwryd the route descends into the beautiful Nant Gwynant with its jewel-like valley lakes (Llyn Gwynant and Llyn Dinas) set amidst pastoral woodlands and lush grazing lands. Although these lakes, like those of Llanberis, occupy hollows deepened by glaciers, there is not much resemblance between these two valleys which skirt Snowdon's rugged flanks. Since they have both been carved from the self-same rocks such an anomaly needs explaining, especially since the Llanberis Pass is a narrow, gaunt and steeply sloping defile while Nant Gwynant is wider and carries its flat valley-floor meadows much more deeply into the mountainland. There are two main reasons. First, Nant Gwynant runs along the general grain of Snowdonia's rock structures while the Llanberis Pass cuts across them. When a carpenter needs to work lengthwise along the grain of a wooden plank he takes a plane, but to rip across the grain of the plank's width, he will need a harsher tool, such as a saw. By analogy, so it is with nature, for rivers and ice have found it easier to work along the grain (from NE to SW), while to make the narrow saw cut of the Llanberis Pass across the mountain crestline necessitated the abrasive powers of an all-enveloping ice sheet, for no pre-glacial river on its own had managed to achieve such a breach (from SE to NW). The second reason for the valley contrasts depends on the volume of glacier ice which Snowdon itself contributed to its skirting valleys. Its eastern flanks produced a relatively small amount of ice in the surprisingly small Cwm Glas (in contrast to the extensive suite of cirques which front northeastwards on to Nant

Ffrancon) (see Walk 3). By comparison, Snowdon's southern slopes spawned enormous glaciers from the gigantic glacial amphitheatres above Cwm Dyli (see Walk 2) and at Cwm Tregalan (see Walk 4). The combined power of these glaciers helped to over-deepen and widen Nant Gwynant. The legacy of their erosive force can best be appreciated at a car

🅿 ⛷

park and viewing point one mile (1.6 km) down the valley. Here is Snowdon with all its trappings, its southern slopes hacked into awesome hollows by relentless glacial tools to give a veritable Alpine scene. Imagine the plunging icefall which once descended from Cwm Dyli and has now been replaced by Glaslyn's cascading torrent. But even the torrent is now a shadow of its former self for most of its waters have been confined to the indignity of metal pipes which sweep down the slope of Cwm Dyli to drive the turbines of Snowdonia's oldest power station.

Bethania 🅿 WC 🅿
Ø. Walk 4

Far ahead, beyond Bethania (Walk 4), is the village of Beddgelert, huddled below the forested peak of Moel Hebog where Owain Glyndwr hid in a cave after rebelling against Henry IV in 1400.

Beddgelert 🅿 WC 🅿
Ø ☕ 🍴 🛏. Walk 6.
Early closing
Wednesday. Turn
left over bridge
on A498
[Porthmadog >]

Beyond the Aberglaslyn Pass (a picturesque defile described in Walk 6) your route leaves the mountains and threads between forested cliffs and reedy marshlands en route to Tremadog. Although you are still seven miles (11.2 km) from the sea the mossy rock faces on your right are old sea cliffs, while the wooded knolls rising abruptly from the Glaslyn marshes are former islands, as the names Ynysferlas and Ynysfawr denote. You may wonder if the Glaslyn estuary has silted up naturally, like that of the Dee farther north. The truth is that the 10 000 acres of Traeth Mawr were reclaimed by William Madocks early in the 19th century following the construction of the Porthmadog embankment. Today the embankment carries a busy road and affords an excellent view of Snowdon. Modern conservationists thought so highly of this scenic tract they insisted that £4 million be spent laying cables underground to protect its view from the intrusion of electricity pylons.

Tremadog 🅿 WC Ø
🍴. Follow A498 (not
Porthmadog) and
bear right on A487
[Caernarfon >]

Stop for a moment in the square of Tremadog, planned by Mr Madocks as a major town to capture the cross-channel trade to Ireland before it was decided to take the traffic along the A5 and through Holyhead instead. Overhanging the main street are a series of beetling cliffs, and they too were sea cliffs less than 200 years ago. Skirting the base of the cliffs are rock aprons formed by the

*Central mountains and western valleys*  57

accumulation of falling stones over countless centuries. Since a thick woodland has become established on these aprons many observers, including Mr Madocks, believed that the rock faces had stopped peeling away and that the aprons had become stabilised. How wrong they were, for in recent years slabs of rock fell on to a house and demolished it. Remedial measures, costing millions of pounds, were hastily undertaken and you can see the reinforced concrete ramps, bars, bolts, steel wires and mesh draped all over the offending precipice. Man had again underestimated the fact that nature works on remorselessly, albeit at a slow pace. It should have been realised that part of Tremadog had been sited in a danger zone.

Penmorfa ⌀. Bear right on by-road at far end of village [Golan >]

At Penmorfa ('head of the marsh') your route at last abandons the main roads and takes to the undulating by-roads. After a few miles you may care to visit the woollen mill, sited as always where a mountain torrent reaches the lowlands with

Brynkir Woollen Mill ℙ. After ¼ mile (0.25 km) bear right for Cwm Pennant

sufficient force to drive the old water wheels. This same lane twists down into the wooded valley of the Afon Dwyfor ('big water') which glides gently out from the hidden valley of Cwm Pennant. As

After crossing river turn right at T-junction

you follow this attractive river upstream it is not long before the valley appears to be completely blocked by a rocky buttress jutting out abruptly from the right-hand valley side. This is Craig Isallt, another example of a band of very hard rock, formed many millions of years ago as molten lava forced its way between the layers of shales and gritstones. Unlike Dinas Mot (see p. 55), which it resembles, the tough 'meat' in this 'sandwich' has lost its upper layer of 'bread' as the overlying rocks have been completely worn away. Nevertheless, the resistant rock band has withstood the battering of the valley glacier which was forced to over-ride its ramp, smoothing its northern slope into deep glacial grooves and plucking gigantic blocks from its southern face to create the cliffs which overlook the bridge. How then did the river break through the barrier? Has its downcutting been more effective than the glacier's grinding? Probably not, for the gorge at Gyfyng is a small-scale edition of the Aberglaslyn Pass (see Walk 6) and was probably formed in the same way by a stream running beneath the glacier. Such a stream was given its

(Opposite) **Cliffs overhanging the tiny town of Tremadog: note the safeguards (top right) to prevent further rockfalls**

Drive into Cwm Pennant ✇ – return on same road but carry straight on when reaching T-junction (see above) and rejoin A487 at Dolbenmaen. Turn right [Caernarfon >]

extra cutting powers because of the considerable pressure exerted by the overlying ice.

Once past the barrier, the pastoral vale of Cwm Pennant is a haven of peace. Its combination of encircling mountain summits, verdant pastures, sheep farms and meandering river encapsulates all that is best in Snowdonia's scenic heritage. It is a place to relax, to picnic on the river bank, or simply to commune with nature. Cwm Pennant also illustrates how upfolds are often worn down into valleys. When the Snowdonian crustal rocks were crumpled into gigantic folds by Earth movements, more than 400 million years ago, a major upfold existed here. But because the rocks were arched their joints were prised open to the sky and the elements soon began to pick away at this weakness in the crestline of the arch. Millions of years of this constant attack have worn down the entire arch until it has become a valley, leaving only the tilted remnants of the rock layers along the valley sides. You can see them now as horizontal benches running one above the other all the way up Cwm Pennant. To think that this gentle river has carried most of that debris away to the Irish Sea; no wonder it is called the Big Water.

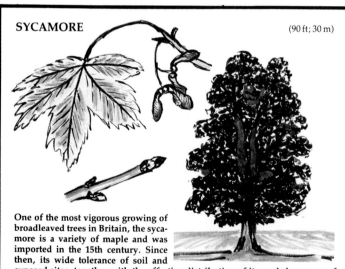

## SYCAMORE

(90 ft; 30 m)

One of the most vigorous growing of broadleaved trees in Britain, the sycamore is a variety of maple and was imported in the 15th century. Since then, its wide tolerance of soil and exposed sites, together with the effective distribution of its seeds by means of 'helicopter keys' has enabled it to spread widely. It has large, pointed leaves that provide a dense shade throughout summer. Unfortunately, unlike the maples in North America, the leaves do not turn scarlet in autumn but merely fade to a yellow–brown.

At Dolbenmaen turn right on to by-road running parallel with A487. After 5 miles (8 km) rejoin A487 at Llanllyfni. Turn right [Caernarfon >]

A few miles beyond the Cwm Pennant diversion your route passes through a very different landscape, a confusion of tiny hills and deep, marshy hollows. One of these, Cors Graianog ('marsh gravel'), neatly explains the way in which it was formed. During the final stages of the Ice Age the mountain glaciers had surged out of the uplands to bury the lowland plains, but in time, as the climate slowly warmed, these far-flung tongues of ice began to melt. As they wasted away an enormous volume of water swilled around these foothills, carrying huge quantities of glacial rubbish that had been worn away from the uplands. Temporary lakes became quickly infilled with thick layers of sand and gravel which, occasionally, buried large chunks of ice, preserving them from the immediate surface melting. Many years later, of course, even the buried ice remnants melted, causing the overlying gravels to collapse into the ensuing voids to form surface hollows. The broad gap of Pant glass ('green hollow') is littered with these marshy hollows while the intervening mounds are constantly being worked for their gravel and sand resources. The extraction companies have cleverly converted British Rail's dismantled railway track into a road for sole use of their heavy lorries, thereby avoiding the urban settlements en route to Caernarfon.

Pen-y-Groes 🅿 🍴. Turn right on B4418

Many of these small towns of western Snowdonia (e.g. Pen-y-Groes and Nantlle) grew up to house the slate quarrymen of the Nantlle valley, for you are now re-entering the slate belt. But look upslope to the stone-walled field patterns and you can discern a network of tiny plots and scattered houses mantling these foothills. This pattern represents the way in which the 19th-century quarrymen also carved out small-holdings from the barren common land in order to supplement their meagre income. Such settlements are a familiar site among the quarry-scarred upland margins, each with their collection of chapels and biblical place names. Nantlle quarries, which once exported their slate on railways constructed by the Stephensons in 1828, are now abandoned, their derelict refuse tips overlooking the beautiful lake of Llyn Nantlle Uchaf. Pause awhile hereabouts, for the lake provides a wonderful foreground for yet another photograph of Snowdon. This view of the summit shows the mountain virtually unsullied by glacial erosion. In contrast to its eastern and southern faces Snowdon's western slopes are almost devoid of glacial hollows, reflecting the

Llyn Nantlle Uchaf.

mechanics of cwm formation discussed on p. 7.

Slate quarrying was not the only occupation of this western valley for in its upper reaches centuries of copper mining have left their imprint. Tradition has it that the Romans won copper here, but more accurately documented is the arrival of the Cornish miners in 1761 and the Anglesey workers in the 1830s after the decline of their world renowned Parys mine. The rich metalliferous vein resulted from the infusion of chemical fluids and vapours through the crustal rocks, associated with the bubbling cauldron of molten rock far below the surface. This deep-seated mass cooled into a granite which has now been unroofed as its overlying rocks have been subjected to millions of years of wear. The great bulk of Mynydd Mawr ('big mountain') to the north of the valley is the resulting eminence. This granite hump is sometimes known as the Elephant Mountain because of its distinctive rounded shape when viewed from the north. Its southern slope, however, has been chopped abruptly by a glacial axe, with Craig-y-bera ('the kite's crag') being another example of an ice-steepened cliff. The same glacier, which ploughed westwards from the Snowdon massif, broke through the head of this western valley to create the narrow pass of Drws-y-coed ('doorway to the woods'), although it was unable completely to obliterate the small but conspicuous granite knob of Clogwyn-y-garreg that sits squarely in the highest point of the breach. Drws-y-coed may appear to be an aptly chosen name, for east of the crest lie the far-reaching forestry plantations of Beddgelert Forest. There is reason to believe, however, that the name refers to the former natural woodlands which flourished in the Nantlle valley before the depradations of industry had reduced them to a few scattered remnants, long before the Forestry Commission had introduced their exotic conifers around Beddgelert.

Before leaving this high pass and coasting down to Rhyd Ddu, you may care to make a final stop to visit Llyn-y-dywarchen ('the lake of the sod'), a water body perched curiously in a glacially scooped hollow at the top of the pass. The odd name is derived from well documented historic records of a floating island driven from end to end by the force of the wind. Several earlier writers

(Opposite) **Snowdon from Llyn Nantlle Uchaf**

*Central mountains and western valleys* 63

claim to have seen this phenomenon, when a floating mass of peat, possibly buoyed up by bubbles of marsh gas, is alleged to have detached itself from the shore, occasionally carrying away startled livestock. You may judge for yourself the reliability of such reports.

Rhyd Ddu [P0] 🅿 🚱.
Turn left on A4085
[Caernarfon >]

From this point the route returns directly to Caernarfon along the line of a Roman road, skirting the deep valley lake of Llyn Cwellyn, the attractive Hafodty gardens near the ancient Nant Mill and passing beneath the sweeping slopes of Moel Eilio ('bare hill') scarred by its former iron ore workings.

# 3   The southern valleys, moorlands and forests
## Porthmadog–Blaenau Ffestiniog–Dolwyddelan– Penmachno–Ffestiniog–Porthmadog

*Introduction*

Apart from the rugged group of heavily quarried slaty mountains encircling Blaenau Ffestiniog, the southern landscapes are gentler and more wooded than those of northern, eastern and western Snowdonia. No high, spiring peaks, no deep glacial troughs or vertiginous precipices will be seen on this drive. Instead, it includes landscapes of subtle and intricate detail, some hidden lakes and secluded valleys, several sudden, surprising vistas and, above all, a number of Man's monumental works. If you are especially interested in industrial archaeology or in modern technology then you can spend a very informative day, but there is also plenty to do for the younger members of the family, good picnic spots and plenty of beautiful scenery.

Porthmadog 🅿 [P0]
wc ⊘ 🚲 🏨 ♥ 🚱 M.
Early closing
Wednesday. For
maritime museum
see Appendix

About half the route is away from the main tourist haunts and there are so many things to see it is best to allow a full day for the excursion. The drive starts at Porthmadog and the distance is about 55 miles (88 km).

*The route*

From Porthmadog
take A487 across
embankment (Toll
gate at east end)

The road starts across the remarkable Porthmadog embankment, constructed against all odds by William Madocks between 1808 and 1814; it was as much a battle against time and debt as against the Glaslyn river floods and storms from the Irish Sea. The Ffestiniog Railway also came this way in 1836

(Opposite) **Drws-y-coed Pass, where glaciers have been unable to destroy the granite knob of Clogwyn-y-garreg**

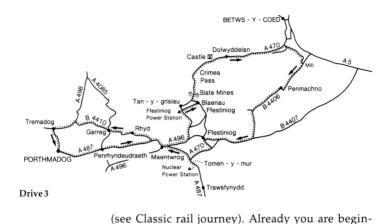

**Drive 3**

Penrhyndeudraeth
**P** **wc** ⊘ ⊕ 🅿.
Portmeirion is
nearby (see
Appendix).
Continue on A487
to Maentwrog **P** 🅿o
⊘. Bear left on A496
[Blaenau
Ffestiniog >]

(see Classic rail journey). Already you are beginning to see the way in which engineers and
industrialists began their dramatic alteration of
Snowdonia's natural scenery, an impact which still
continues. As you cross the embankment look left
across the reedy marshlands of Traeth Mawr ('large
beach') and try to visualise what it must have
looked like some 200 years ago when this was a
stretch of open seawater, reflecting the stately cone
of Snowdon. A few miles beyond Penrhyndeudraeth the road descends into the beautifully
wooded Vale of Ffestiniog, the inner end of the
unspoilt sandy estuary of Traeth Bach ('little
beach'). Compare the two estuarine landscapes, for
Traeth Mawr is more like a Dutch polder while
Traeth Bach is a true Welsh coastal valley with its
untrammelled tidal river swinging gracefully from
side to side of this narrow glacial trough. The thick
woodlands which blanket the sides of the Vale are
largely deciduous and include a few remnants of
Snowdonia's primeval forest of oak, ash and alder.
Like most glacial troughs, the rocky floor is now
deeply buried by thick layers of gravel, sand and
mud, laid down at different times; first by glaciers,
then in this case by an invasion of the sea and
finally by the Afon·Dwyryd, its principal river.
Because of this fertile green floor and the climbing
woodlands of its sides it is sometimes difficult to
think of the Vale of Ffestiniog as a product of ice
sheets because the bare scoured rocks are hidden
from view unlike those of the Nant Ffrancon and
Llanberis Pass. But once you've turned northwards

After 1¼ miles (2 km)
carry straight on
(B4414) (*not* right for
Blaenau Ffestiniog
(A496))

up the wooded gorge of the Afon Goedol a vastly
different prospect awaits you. Trees virtually disappear, subordinated to a bare rocky landscape
savaged by both glaciers and industry.

Tan-y-Grisiau.
Ffestiniog power
station 🅿 ⌀
(entrance opposite
turning to Blaenau
Ffestiniog)

Before entering the town of Blaenau Ffestiniog you should make a particular point of visiting the hydro-electric power station at Tan-y-Grisiau. It is remarkable ingenuity to utilise nature's gifts in the service of mankind. The Ffestiniog scheme, opened in 1963, was Wales' first pumped storage project and was later to be copied by the vastly bigger Dinorwig scheme at Llanberis. By building a dam across the lip of a high, glacially scoured armchair hollow (or cwm), 1600 feet (488 m) up in the Moelwyn mountains the tiny lake was converted into the Llyn Stwlan reservoir. When daytime electricity demands are high, water is released down massive underground pipes to drive the power station turbines before being fed into the larger artificial lake of Tan-y-Grisiau. At night, when surplus power is available (because electricity cannot be properly stored) the water is pumped back to the upper lake ready for use next day. You can either tour the power station, take the bus up to Stwlan Dam or simply visit the information centre (see Appendix). The hairpin bends up to Stwlan make this the most spectacular road in Wales and the view from the top is certainly worth the drive.

Blaenau Ffestiniog
🅿 📵 wc ⌀ 🏠 🍴 ♿
ℹ. Early closing
Thursday. For
museums see
Appendix

From the power station entrance take the nearest road into Blaenau Ffestiniog and you will pass into a different world. This sturdy, grey town is almost encircled by countless millions of tons of slate waste: this is the reason why it is excluded from the national park. It looks desolate on an overcast or wet day but hides some remarkable surprises if you care to look with an informed eye. Before visiting the slate workings, you will see ahead of you, on crossing the main railway bridge, an almost vertical rock face, overhanging the properties at the western end of the high street, indeed, the local café is called the Hanging Rock Café. And hang the rock certainly does – literally! Or at least it did, until 1982 when the local council decided that the glacially oversteepened rock face was too dangerous to leave any longer. Since the 19th century, stout metal chains have held the frost-shattered blocks in position. Had nature been allowed to run its course these blocks would have fallen long ago to create a pile of scree at the cliff foot. How foolish it was to extend the Victorian town into such a hazardous location. The very cold winter of 1981–2 caused a considerably greater degree of splitting and sliding of the unstable cliff face and remedial measures were quickly undertaken to buttress the precipice and avoid a

*Southern valleys, moorlands and forests* 67

The dangerous crag above the main street of Blaenau Ffestiniog, showing safety measures being implemented

disastrous collapse. You may judge the magnitude of the multi-million pound scheme, while en route to the neighbouring slate excavations.

You now have a choice, to visit either the Gloddfa Ganol, which is the world's largest slate mine or the Llechwedd Slate Caverns where you can go underground on two separate railways. Both show the difficult and hazardous working

*Drives* 68

conditions of the now virtually defunct industry and an instructive couple of hours can easily be spent here especially if it's raining, for you can stay under cover (see Appendix). One interesting point is that at Blaenau Ffestiniog the slaty rocks are both younger and alternate more rapidly with layers of volcanic rocks than those at Bethesda and Dinorwig. Thus, instead of the simple opencast quarries of the latter, the Ffestiniog slates had to be mined underground, with the 'miners' following the steeply dipping and contorted 'seams' deep into the earth.

A470 [Dolwyddelan, Betws-y-Coed >]
🚗 ⚜

The road northwards, over the so-called Crimea Pass, returns once more to Snowdonia's pastoral calm leaving behind the scarred and disfigured landscape. But you still cannot escape the human imprint. Mile after mile of forestry plantation blankets the valley sides and the mountain slopes all the way to Betws-y-Coed. Here, on these bleak and deserted moorlands, the Forestry Commission have methodically converted upland sheep farms into a sea of dark green conifers. Occasional glimpses of the high, mountainous heartland can be seen to the north; even Snowdon appears fleetingly to the left of Moel Siabod's conical peak which itself dominates the skyline for the next few miles.

Dolwyddelan 🅿 **WC**
🏰 🚽 ♿ ☎. Early closing Thursday. Admission to castle free (Open week-days 9.30–dusk)

At about the half-way point between Blaenau Ffestiniog and Betws-y-Coed the gaunt square keep of Dolwyddelan castle comes into view. This 12th-century Welsh castle, safe in the innermost recesses of the uplands, was the headquarters of the Welsh princes when they fought the English invading armies.

You have now left the high moorlands and for the next few miles both road and railway follow the floor of the narrow Lledr valley. Although the road twists and switchbacks, the railway is forced to tunnel through the valleyside ridges and spurs, as both road and rail attempt to keep well above the flood plain of the Lledr. Near Dolwyddelan the river meanders gently for about seven miles (11.2 km) descending a mere 400 feet (120 m) until it crosses beneath the large railway viaduct at Cethin's Bridge. In the upstream reaches hayfields and marshy tracts jostle with each other on the flat valley floor and the presence of artificial river embankments (dykes) in places suggests that the river is prone to flooding. By Cethin's Bridge, however, the flat valley floor has narrowed and disappeared while the lazy current has quickened

*Southern valleys, moorlands and forests* 69

**Slate quarries at Blaenau Ffestiniog**

its pace as the Lledr begins to leap and bounce over a rocky floor once again, because the gradient has suddenly steepened. Unlike the neighbouring Llugwy and Machno rivers and the trunk stream of the Conwy, the Lledr is devoid of waterfalls or spectacular gorges where it empties into the Conwy valley. It is difficult to explain this anomaly for it crosses the same type of alternating shales, sandstones and volcanic rocks as do the other rivers. But if you want to see the spectacular gorges and waterfalls hereabouts why not take Walk 5.

Once you reach sight of the Conwy valley you don't have to make the long detour across Pont-yr-afanc and back southwards on the A5 trunk road,

After 4¼ miles (6.8 km) on A470 from Dolwyddelan turn right over small stone bridge on to by-road along banks of river Conwy

Penmachno Woollen
Mill ▣. See
Appendix. Turn
right on B4406
[Penmachno >]

for there is a quicker way. The short-cut not only
avoids the holiday traffic but also gives you a
chance to see a typical Welsh water mill at work
and provides an opportunity to browse through its
wares on sale in the shop. It is a picturesque spot
and a good shady place to stop for a picnic tea if it's
a hot day. The gracefully arched canopies of the
trees, the romantic packhorse bridge (the so-called
Roman Bridge) and the tumbling waters also give
many opportunities to indulge your photographic
skills.

Penmachno ⌀ ▣ ▣.
Continue on B4406
[Ffestiniog >] and
after 5 miles (8 km)
turn right at T-
junction on to B4407
[Ffestiniog >]

The next four miles (6.4 km) along the flat-
floored Machno valley and through the tiny slate
quarrymen's village of Penmachno, is a repeat
performance of the Lledr valley scene, but this time
without the railway. Both the Machno and Lledr
valleys are occasionally scarred with small abandoned slate workings to remind you that you are
still passing through slaty and shaly rocks. Their
presence and the dearth of the Snowdonian volcanic rock layers means that in this area there are
no great differences in the hardness of the various
rock layers. Thus, nearly all the rocks hereabouts
have worn down uniformly to give a series of
undulating plateaux into which the rivers have
cut very similar valleys. This rather monotonous
plateau landscape is best seen when you have
climbed steeply out of the forested Machno valley
and crossed the first cattle grid onto the open
moorland of Migneint.

Migneint ('swampy place') lives up to its name,
for the 1500 foot (457 m) moorland plateau is a
desolate, boggy and lonely place. It is a wilderness
of heathery peat, crossed by fleeting cloud shadows and inhabited only by sheep, grouse, snipe
and curlew. It is also the source of many streams,
foremost of which is the Conwy, starting from its
solitary lake about one mile (1.6 km) east of your
route. Away to the south-east the rugged peaks of
Arenig Fawr and Arenig Fach rise dramatically
more than 1000 feet (300 m) above the rolling
plateau. Not surprisingly, they indicate a change of
rock type for there, to the south, a lengthy exposure
of the hard Snowdonian volcanic rocks reappears.
There is one interesting point worth making about
the featureless Migneint plateau: during the Ice
Age it became the centre of the North Welsh ice
cap. Here, cradled between the high peaks of the
Arenigs and those of the northern mountains
around Snowdon, the ice cap reached its greatest
thickness before moving radially outwards in all

*Southern valleys, moorlands and forests*   71

direction's. Some of its glaciers reached the English Plain at Shrewsbury, others drove far west to the Llyn Peninsula; those driving northwards were responsible for breaching the middle part of Snowdonia's backbone at Ogwen and Pen-y-Pass (see Drive 2).

After joining the Bala-Ffestiniog road (B4391) a surprise awaits you. The plateau edge drops suddenly away, creating a dramatic waterfall known as Rhaeadr-y-Cwm and giving a good view of the Vale of Ffestiniog. Like most precipitous steps in the landscape, rocks of different hardness are brought together and streams are able to excavate one more easily than the other. This waterfall is no exception, for the stream plunges over a particularly resistant intrusion of dolerite, injected as a fluid lava flow between the layers of gritstone millions of years ago but now uncovered by the ravages of weather and stream action. The route continues down into Ffestiniog.

Not far to the south, cradled by the bulky gritstone mountains, is the broad but shallow Trawsfynydd Lake. At its northern end stands another of Man's mighty artifacts: the Trawsfynydd nuclear power station, the only one to be located in a British national park. You may well ask what the reasons are for such a location. The two most important are, distance from large urban population centres and a constant supply of water for cooling purposes. Trawsfynydd lake had already been artificially expanded to supply a sufficient head of water for the tiny pre-war hydro-electric power station at Maentwrog on the floor of the Vale of Ffestiniog. But in 1965 the lake was put to even sterner uses by the CEGB. Fears were originally expressed that the warmer water fed out into the lake, after having fulfilled its cooling purpose, would have serious effects on the marine life and on the surrounding vegetation. This concern has now been shown to be unfounded. If you do not wish to visit the power station there is a nature trail to enjoy at the northern end of the lake, or the nearby Roman fort of Tomen-y-Mur on the hillside above the main road.

The return journey can be made directly to Porthmadog via the main A487 trunk road, but for those desirous of a more picturesque, if slower, route why not follow the beautiful secondary road through Rhyd. It starts at the Oakley Arms at Tan-y-bwlch, on the floor of the Vale of Ffestiniog, and climbs through thick broadleaf forest before

Turn right on to B4391 [Ffestiniog >]. After 8 miles (12.8 km) **P** on left for ⚲

Ffestiniog **P** **wc** **PO** ∅ ⛽ ⛫. Early closing Thursday. Turn left on A470 [Dolgellau >] and drive 1 mile (1.6 km) to power station

From nuclear power station, return 1 mile (1.6 km) on A470 then A487 [Porthmadog >]. For Tomen-y-Mur turn first right off A470, ½ mile (0.8 km) north of power station entrance (*not* Ffestiniog road)

Tan-y-bwlch ⛫. Turn right on B4410 [Rhyd >]

Llyn Mair 🅿️.
Picnic site
reaching the jewel-like lake of Llyn Mair embowered in its oak and ashwoods. This tiny artificially dammed hollow of placid water is a haven of peace, with a picnic site, car park and nature trail all discreetly fitted into the idyllic scene. It is a place to relax after the long drive and somewhere for the children to play safely before returning to Porthmadog and its bustling streets. The road twists and switchbacks down to the marshy plain of Traeth Mawr, but note the devastated area of woodland near Rhyd, where thousands of dead trees bear silent testimony to a forest fire started a few years

Garreg 🔄 🖉. Cross
A4085. Continue on
B4410 and in 2 miles
(3.2 km) turn left at
T-junction on A498.
Prenteg 🔄 🖉
[Tremadog >]
ago by a careless visitor. From Garreg, on the marshy floor of the old seabed, the easiest (and cheapest, since it avoids the toll) route is across the marsh to Prenteg and thence to Tremadog. Note how the very straight middle section of the road, just prior to crossing the Glaslyn river at Pont Croesor, follows the embankment of an old railway track: the same one that snakes through the Aberglaslyn Pass (see Walk 6). So you return to Porthmadog as you left it, on an artificial earthwork constructed by modern engineers in this age-old scenery.

**ROWAN**
(50–65 ft; 15–20 m)

This small tree is often called the mountain ash because of its tolerance of exposed upland sites and its pattern of finely toothed oblong leaflets. However, it is not even slightly related to the lowland ash. The rowan is particularly conspicuous because of its smooth, grey, horizontally scarred bark, its ascending branches and its clusters of scarlet berries.

(Opposite) **The picnic site at Llyn Mair**

# Walks of mountain, valley and coast

## Dry days

## 1  The Blacklands: the Dolgarrog area

Full day

*Introduction*
This walk takes you off the main tourist routes into the unfrequented plateaux of eastern Snowdonia. Here the lonely glacial hollows and dark, brooding lakes are hemmed in by beetling crags. Sullen streams crawl across black peaty moorlands before suddenly plunging in surging cascades and rapids down the forested cliffs of the Conwy valley, there to impinge upon the mainstream of civilisation with its attendant buzz of traffic and hum of machinery. It is a walk in which solitude prevails, where you can momentarily escape into a mountain wilderness, disturbed only by the plaintive bleating of sheep, the sigh of the wind and the haunting call of the curlew.

*The walk*
Since this is a lengthy (4–5 hours) walk, at elevations of 1000 to 1200 feet (300–360 m), it is best to attempt it on a dry day, even if the summits are cloud-capped. It is an easy walk apart from the initial ascent and final descent but the steepness of these may well deter young children. It will probably be wet underfoot so boots or wellingtons are essential. For the first hour you follow a metalled road so do beware of traffic on the blind bends. A careful study of place names along the way will give a remarkably clear explanation of the landscape and illustrate in part why the walk is entitled the *blacklands*. If you want a short walk only, follow 1, 2 and 4 by keeping to the road.

*The route*

1 ⬅ From Conwy B5106 south, or from Betws-y-Coed B5106 north to Tal-y-Bont 🅿

As soon as you leave the main valley road at Tal-y-Bont ('end of the bridge') the lane begins to steepen. As you pass beneath the power lines take a breather and look back at the view. The farm below you is Gwern-y-felin ('mill of the marsh') suggesting that the tumbling waters of the adjacent Afon Dulyn were once harnessed to turn the

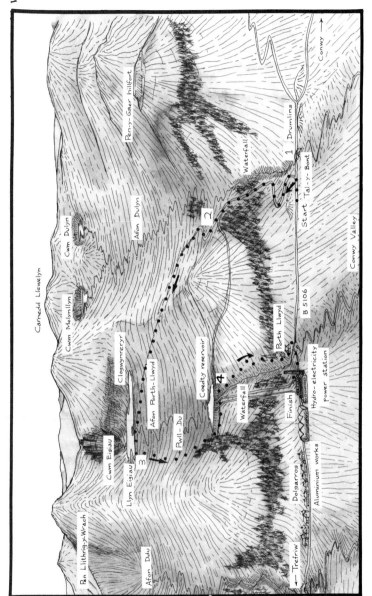

Carnedd Llewelyn

Pen-y-Gaer hillfort

Cwm Dulyn

Afon Dulyn

Cwm Melynllyn

Claswynerayr

Cwm Eigiau

Afon Porth-Llwyd

Pen Llithrig-y-Wrach

Llyn Eigiau

Pwll-Du

Coedty reservoir

Afon Ddu

Trefriw

Dolgarrog

Aluminium works

Hydro-electricity Power Station

Waterfall

Finish

Porth Llwyd

B 5106

Waterfall

Drumlins

Start Tal-y-Bont

Conwy Valley

Conwy

1

2

3

4

wheels of a former mill. Away to the right an electricity pylon stands on a whale-backed grassy hill. To the left the main valley road snakes through a couple of similar hills at Castell. These low hillocks are termed 'drumlins', formed when the Conwy valley glacier drove northwards for the last time, some 20 000 years ago. The rocky debris and rubbish (known as 'boulder clay') that it had dumped during a previous advance, was ice moulded into smooth elongated domes. Drumlins are common in the lowlands of Ireland, Scotland and North of England but you won't see many in mountainous North Wales, only in lowland Anglesey.

Push on up the very steep gradient past the aptly named house Tan'r allt ('under the wooded hill-side'). It's probably no consolation to be told that the steep cliffs are caused by a thick layer of volcanic rock which cap the underlying softer slates and mudstones. You may be so out of breath that you do not care to know that the Conwy glacier gouged out these less resistant sedimentary rocks of the valley floor thereby oversteepening the valley sides. Away to the right a constant roar of falling water accompanies your climb. The Afon Dulyn is leaping down these precipitous slopes and a path leads off down to a footbridge in the wooded gorge. The Conwy valley lies at your feet, scoured out over millions of years by rivers and finally by glaciers along the line of a massive fracture (termed a fault) which split the older, harder rocks of Snowdonia from the younger, less resistant rocks to the east. To the west lie the mountains and dark moorlands; to the east the bright patchwork of Clwyd's undulating farm-lands and forested hills, the two divided by the watery green trench of the Conwy. Closer to, across the Afon Dulyn, the ramparts of an Iron Age hillfort, Pen-y-Gaer, command the hillslope (see p. 13).

**2** Follow road up zig-zags to ⚡ Carreg-y-fford ('road on the rock'); above Carreg-y-ffordd take right fork

For the next 3½ miles (5.6 km) your walk is across rolling treeless moorland, seamed with stone walls and broken by occasional rocky outcrops. The sombre and featureless tracts of rushy pasture give this plateauland a sense of desolation, and the mountain precipices stand back as if tempting you onwards to discover their secrets. And this solitary place does have secrets. Its abandoned farmsteads could tell tales of upland toil on stony soils or

(Opposite) **The lonely hollow of Cwm Eigiau**

boggy pastures, generally in harsh weather, miles from the comfortable lowlands whose villagers sat snugly at the mountain foot forgetful of the lonely dwellings in the rain-drenched uplands. But one terrible night the roles were temporarily reversed, as you will soon discover.

To your right the long rocky ridge, jutting north from the frowning cliffs behind Llyn Eigiau, was once alive with these hardy sheep and cattle farmers living in Hafod-y-garreg ('summer dwelling on the rock'), Hafod-fach ('smaller summer dwelling'), Ty'n-rhos ('house on the moor') or in Tal-y-llyn ('house at the end of the lake'). Today, all are ruined but their earliest inhabitants may once have marvelled at the eagles, now long departed, after which the neighbouring crags were named (Clogwynyreryr; 'eagles' cliff'). From 1907 to 1910 their descendants would have seen Llyn Eigiau's waters artificially raised behind a concrete dam in order to supplement the natural catchment of the Afon Porth-llwyd whose waters drive the electricity-generating turbines at Dolgarrog in Conwy's vale. If you look at the lake shores you will find that they consist of peat sitting on thick boulder clay. The original dam was built upon these poorly consolidated materials not upon solid rock. Imagine yourself here on a stormy night with waves pounding at the dam and scouring away at its foundations. 2 November, 1925 was such a night, and the lake waters, swollen by weeks of heavy rain, finally undermined the retaining wall and broke it down. The breach is still visible to the right of the modern outlet. A staggering 3 million cubic metres of water suddenly surged along the tiny upland valley, tearing out massive boulders from the glacial clay. The tiny subsidiary reservoir at Coedty, lower downstream, was demolished before the destructive wall of water plunged over the Conwy valley shoulder. Never before or since has this mountain stream had such power. For a short time its energy was sufficient to carry 500 tonne boulders, that normally only a glacier would be capable of transporting. It was this lethal cargo that crashed down on to the unsuspecting village of Porth-llwyd at the foot of the gorge. This settlement, where 16 died, now lies buried beneath an enormous debris fan, which you will see at the end of your walk. During the first hour the tiny stream's discharge shot up to almost half that of a flood-swollen Mississippi, itself one of the world's mightiest rivers!

**3** Track starts short way up hillside near a mountain rescue telephone. Keep river to your left and follow former tramway track

As you follow the track back north eastwards, away from the infamous lake, pondering the magnitude of that tragic event, the first inhabited farm is Pwll-du ('black pool'). Its name is one of many hereabouts suggesting that these could usefully be called the 'blacklands'. Look back to the dark rugged skyline perhaps shrouded in cloud or starkly silhouetted against the midday sun; the valley-floor soils are peaty, staining the river waters after rain and turning them into turgid black pools; the hillside ahead is termed Cae du ('black field') named, perhaps, from its exposed black mudstones; above all the lowering clouds are beginning to shroud the dark, shaded hollows from which the rivers emanate. Consider the river names: to the north flows the Afon Dulyn ('the river from the black lake'), while in the next valley south is the Afon Ddu ('the black river'). Below the Coedty reservoir the Afon Porth-llwyd itself wanders past the ruined farm of Ffrith-ddu ('the black mountain pasture'). It is as if the very landscape echoes the despair of that catastrophic flood.

A few steps east of Pwll-du farm a bridge spans a water course, but this is no ordinary stream. You would have every right to be puzzled, for the water seems to defy the normal laws of nature; instead of flowing eastwards down the valley, just like the Afon Porth-llwyd, this one runs *along* the hillside in a westerly direction. You'd be even more puzzled if you were told that these waters come round the hillside from the Afon Ddu. But water runs *along* hillslopes only if the works of man intervene. There has obviously been a considerable alteration of the natural stream catchments hereabouts as part of the measures, mentioned above, to supplement the Afon Porth-llwyd's potential to generate hydro-electricity. Thus, artificial channels (termed 'leats') have been constructed along the hillsides to bring water from neighbouring valleys into the Coedty reservoir. This in turn acts as a 'header tank' before its regulated supply is led away in those huge black metal pipes which cross the tarmac road at Pont Newydd and then plunge steeply down the wooded hillside to the Dolgarrog power station.

**4** Turn right off road over stile keeping river to your right. Down through fence opening, over stile and through another fence opening. Over wall stile, past cottage and down to gate into lane. Rejoin B5106

Once you've crossed Pont Newydd ('the new bridge') the route follows a steep path down the left bank of the river. It takes you to the lip of the gorge where the river descends in a succession of waterfalls to the valley floor. Because it has been robbed of so much water, however, the descending stream

An artificial water channel and Coedty reservoir above Dolgarrog

is but a shadow of its natural flow. Nevertheless, when you are near the bottom of this steep descent, among those few remnants of Porth-llwyd village that cling to the steep hillside, look back up the gorge and try to visualise the frightful tidal wave that swept down this quiet wooded gorge long ago (the nearby house name 'Ceunant' means 'ravine'). When you reach the main road opposite the power station and its associated aluminium works (see Drive 1) spare a moment to cross back over the stream and take the lane that winds upslope on its southern bank. From there you can wander

(Opposite) **The flood-dumped boulders which buried the village of Porth-llwyd**

through the trees on to the boulder fan and contemplate on the mighty forces which rivers can sometimes unleash. The earliest settlers at Porth-llwyd ('grey port') believed that they had made a wise choice. They sited their village just high enough to avoid dangers from flooding by the Conwy but near enough to use this main river as a means of transport. The grey-stone hamlet would have been centred round a watermill driven by the tumbling cataract of the Afon Porth-llwyd, in much the same way as the woollen mills were located at neighbouring Trefriw (see Drive 1). But in the end the simple mistakes of the construction engineers high in the mountains left these villagers more vulnerable to the vagaries of water than their upland colleagues.

## KESTREL

This is the most frequently seen falcon in Britain, a bird of prey that hovers high above the ground before swooping down to catch voles and other small mammals from open grassland or moor. The kestrel is a beautiful chestnut colour, and the male bird has a blue–grey head and tail.

# 2 The summit of Wales: Snowdon

Full day

## Introduction

At some time during your visit to Snowdonia you will probably feel like ascending a high mountain: why not make it the supreme peak in southern Britain? Snowdon is the highest in Wales, higher than anything in England and is certainly one of Britain's shapeliest summits. This walk is for strong, resolute mountain walkers in fine weather and is not intended for the novice, for young children or the elderly. Under no circumstances should it be attempted in heavy rain or thick mist and certainly not in snowy or icy conditions. If you *must* visit the summit and you are not a good hill walker, then go by train. Before setting off, a few pieces of advice: first, footpath erosion on Snowdon has become a very serious problem, so please help the conservationists, who are improving the drainage and restoring the footpaths, by keeping to the tracks; secondly, car parking at Pen-y-Pass is very limited and expensive, so why not park at the foot of the Llanberis Pass and take a Snowdon Sherpa Bus to the head of the Pass (see Appendix). Remember that adequate climbing boots are necessary; also anoraks and sweaters should be carried, as the weather may change for the worse. Turn back at the Zig-Zags if it deteriorates badly – it is dangerous in mist from there upwards.

## The walk

1 ↩ From Llanberis A4086 south or from Capel Curig A4086 west. Pen-y-Pass 🅿. Alternatively use Snowdon Sherpa Bus (Appendix)

Allow at least 5 hours for the entire journey. Alternatively, take the train up from Llanberis to the summit and walk down (see Appendix for Snowdon Mountain Railway). For a shorter, easier walk follow **1**, **2** and **3** and turn back below Zig-Zags for **5**.

## The route

Since this is the most popular route to the summit, it will probably be thronged with people on a fine day, leaving the Pen-y-Pass car park in droves, so do not expect solitude (some half-million people walk on Snowdon each year). Its popularity is a tribute to the majestic scenery and the attractive shape of the peak from this aspect. As you glimpse its sharp summit cone surrounded by dark precipices which plunge straight into a high level lake, you will feel that you are climbing a real mountain!

2 Path leaves top right-hand corner of 🅿

The path you are following, known as the Pyg track (standing for Pen-y-Gwryd), skirts the northern side of the Tal-y-Llyn ridge. It rises steadily to a break in the ridge, termed Bwlch Moch, and gives many opportunities to look down the spectacular ice-scoured defile of the Llanberis Pass, noting the way in which the ends of the ridges have been

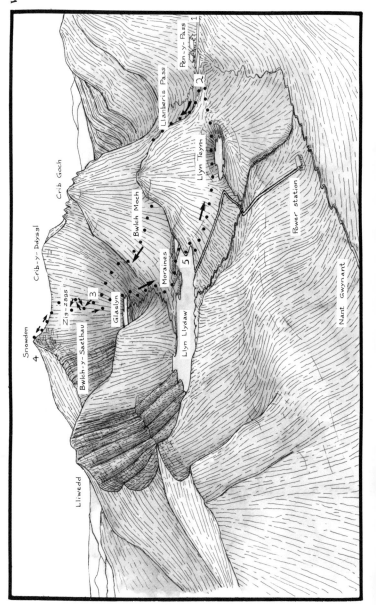

**Pen-y-Pass car park and the start of the Pyg track – Crib Goch rises beyond**

sliced off by a former glacier (see Leisure drive 2).
Look back, also, to the Youth Hostel at Pen-y-Pass
and think about its ideal location. It has not always
been owned by the YHA, for the original building
was founded in 1850 as an inn at the highest point
of the Pass to give shelter to weary travellers on foot
and on horseback.

The gap of Bwlch Moch gives you a chance to halt, catch your breath, after having climbed a brisk 600 feet (182 m), and appreciate the first major panorama. This must be one of Snowdonia's most impressive views and includes the entire Snowdon Horseshoe, the name popularly given to the arc of high summits cradling the steely-blue waters of Llyn Llydaw. Across the lake are the startling cliffs of Lliwedd (Snowdonia's highest precipice); to their right the symmetrical pyramid of Yr Wyddfa (the summit itself); to the right again the gently rounded hump of Crib-y-Ddysgl; and finally, towering almost vertically above your head the mighty serrated ridge of Crib Goch. The group is almost Alpine in appearance, if not in stature, and it does not need much imagination to refill these deep hollows with snow and ice and restore the majesty of the Ice Age. Almost everything you see on this walk is a product of glaciers and frost. These tools have variously shattered, split, heaved, pounded, scraped and polished the solid rocks hereabouts to create this remarkable scene. Try to reconstruct in your mind's eye the domed shape of the Snowdon massif before the Ice Age began and then you will begin to appreciate the enormous amount of material that has been gouged out and shunted off down the adjoining valleys. No wonder there is so much boulder clay on the surrounding lowlands; some of it was carried as far away as Oxford!

For the next two miles the Pyg track traverses along the flank of Crib Goch and you gain height steadily. It gives you an opportunity to view Snowdon's summit cone and to pick out something of its rock structure. You will see that its rocky layers are bent into a gentle downfold, a situation which might strike you as puzzling. Surely upfolds will form the mountains and downfolds the valleys? In most cases the opposite is true because where rocks are bent upwards they open up fissures to the weather so that the rock fragments are easily split and removed. Over millions of years layer after layer is peeled away from the upfolds while the downfolds remain relatively intact because their fractures are squeezed tightly together. Thus, the upfolded rocks are worn into lower areas while the downfolded rocks remain as higher relief, as in the case of Snowdon. Here, the rocks are composed almost entirely of tough lavas, or layers of hardened volcanic ash and other volcanic debris, so that they provide a rugged

**The summit cone of Snowdon from the east**

appearance wherever they have been etched by nature's tools.

Below you the tiny lake of Glaslyn ('green lake') comes into view, its name being derived in part from the staining of its waters from the copper ores which occur on Snowdon's southern flanks. This explains the ruined buildings which you will see more closely on your return. Glaslyn is a fine glacial lake, deeply embowered in an ice-deepened rock hollow (126 feet (38 m) deep) with the summit precipice frowning almost directly above. Note how this cwm 'hangs' above that in which Llyn Llydaw lies, which in turn 'hangs' above the cwm containing Llyn Teyrn (you will see all three from the summit). This forms a glacial staircase in which each of the hollows is separated from its neighbour by a valley step over which icefalls once tumbled, thousands of years ago.

**3** Miners' track and Pyg track join here

The final climb to the summit is now ahead of you, up the notorious Zig-Zags, a steep, heart-pounding slog up the almost vertical backwall of a cwm! But the view from the top is worth the effort. The whole mountain range surrounds you and if you are lucky the visibility will allow you to see westwards to the isolated conical peaks of the Llyn Peninsula, northwards across the mosaic of Anglesey, eastwards across the rolling plateaux of Clwyd, and finally southwards, across the rugged peaks and valleys of southern Snowdonia. If you are really lucky, you may be able to see Ireland, the Isle of Man and the Lake District. Even if visibility is poor you cannot fail to be impressed by the panoply of deep hollows, cliffs, screes, lakes and splintered peaks which make up this fretted view, ragged, torn and tortured but still standing proud as Wales' premier mountain mass.

**4** Summit café **WC** ☕ ⬦ ☎. On descent do *not* walk on railway track. Turn right at first stone monolith, steeply down slope

On the return journey retrace your footsteps to the Zig-Zags, noting the way in which the sawtoothed, pinnacle ridge of Crib Goch lives up to its name of the 'Red Ridge', as it looks just like a cock's comb. Its shattered knife edge, where the backwalls of two cwms have almost intersected, is one of Wales' best examples of a glacially etched knife-edged ridge. But do not attempt to follow that ridge unless you are a skilled mountaineer; your route descends the Zig-Zags all the way down to Glaslyn and the Miners' track.

It is termed the Miners' track to commemorate the large number of copper workers who once trod these steep slopes. The mine was at Glaslyn and the ruined lakeside barracks and waste tips are all that remains of this part of the enterprise. By modern standards it is remarkable to think that at weekends those miners who lived at Beddgelert returned home from Glaslyn by scaling the col (Bwlch-y-Saethau) that you can see in the ridge between Snowdon and Lliwedd, prior to descending the Watkin Path (see Walk 4). The other ruined buildings of this derelict Britannia mine can be seen lower down, at Llyn Llydaw. Not only was the ore carried down from Glaslyn by overhead cableway but also the lake waters themselves were led down a leat to drive the water wheel of the sorting and crushing mills. When the mine was in full production during the 19th century, it is said that Llyn Llydaw was turned a greenish-blue by the copper waste. Shipping the dressed ore across the lake by horse and cart aboard a flimsy raft proved to be a hazardous business and it was not long before the causeway was constructed to speed up the journey to Pen-y-Pass.

5 If causeway is submerged follow left-hand lake shore

All Snowdonia's metal ores were initially deposited by hot vapours and solutions rising from a subterranean lava cauldron deep below the surface. As they permeated the overlying rocks the vapours solidified in the rock's pores and fissures to form mineral veins. These are associated with the white quartz veins which run conspicuously across the slopes hereabouts. If you pick up a piece of white quartz you may see a small fleck of gleaming metal in the rock.

Around Llyn Llydaw's shores you'll also see a number of hummocks of earthy material and at first glance you may think that they are piles of mining waste. In fact, they *are* composed of waste material but were dumped not 100 years ago by miners but more than 10 000 years ago by the glaciers which carved out these gigantic basins. These are glacial 'moraines' deposited by Snowdon's southern glacier as it stood at the lip of Llyn Llydaw's glacial hollow. Glaslyn and Llyn Teyrn, too, have similar hummocky moraines on the outer side of their shores, but these do not dam the lakes which lie in true rock basins. If you look closely at the bare rock surfaces you will discover deep grooves and/or scratches where stones frozen into the base of the ice were once dragged bodily across the bedrock. These were the tools which excavated the enormous hollows through which you are walking. Ice alone is incapable of wearing down a hard rock surface. Thus, when you read of glaciers being responsible for carving cwms and troughs, it is really the work of stones carried along in the sole of the glacier, just as hob-nails in the soles of early climbing boots once wore away the rocky tracks up Snowdon. Today it is rare to see nailed boots in the mountains, so that track erosion by human activity

*Snowdon* 93

should now be less not more. Unfortunately, this is not the case, because of the sheer volume of modern visitors, some disturbing the stones, others taking short-cuts, blocking the culverts with rubbish or trampling the vegetation, all contributing to a degree of footpath erosion that the few early climbers would never have envisaged. It is a remarkable commentary on Snowdon's popularity that damage to the ground surface in the vicinity of the summit has been on such a scale in recent years that serious consideration has been given to limiting the numbers visiting the mountain. It is possible that in a decade there has been as much erosion by human feet as has been achieved by natural processes in about 1000 years.

After passing the double pipeline, which leads the waters of Llyn Llydaw down to the hydro-electric power station of Cwm Dyli on the Gwynant Valley floor, you will skirt the northern shore of Llyn Teyrn, the lowest of the three cwm-lakes along the route. Here, the track leaves the layered volcanic rocks for a short stretch and crosses a tough rock band known as 'dolerite'. The dolerite intruded its molten flow between these existing rock layers, there to cool and solidify into a dark, crystalline sheet. During the cooling process the dolerite split into prismatic shapes which have

---

## NORWAY SPRUCE
(80 ft; 25 m)

The 'Christmas tree' spruce, as it is more commonly known, must be one of the most easily recognised of all trees. The branches are pendulous and dense, grouped in such a way as to make an almost perfect conical shape from the ground to the tip. Each branch carries grass-green needles that strike out singly from the twigs, and cylindrical cones that hang from

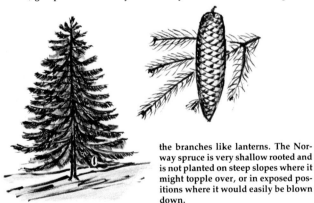

the branches like lanterns. The Norway spruce is very shallow rooted and is not planted on steep slopes where it might topple over, or in exposed positions where it would easily be blown down.

ultimately been exposed and weathered out into columnar rock structures, very similar to the basaltic columns of Fingal's Cave or the Giant's Causeway. You can see these curious 'organ-pipe' columns in the crags across Llyn Teyrn.

From here back to Pen-y-Pass is a gentle stroll along an excellent track, giving you time to give a final thought to the vegetation which clothes the mountains in this heartland. Trees are few and far between, largely because of their early clearance and the way in which sheep grazing has subsequently checked any regeneration of seedlings. Many people believe that the diminishing growth of trees as they are traced up the flanks of Nant Gwynant represents the natural tree line of the region. This is not the case, for where there is artificial or natural protection from grazing, trees will survive, judging by the fine specimens around the Pen-y-Gwryd hotel. In the peaty layers of the mountain hollows ancient tree-stumps are often uncovered, testifying to a thick forest cover up to heights of 2500 feet (760 m) on all but the most exposed rocky faces in former times, although the climate was probably warmer and drier then. You may also be struck by the changes in colour of the grasslands. Where so-called acid rocks create sour soils the grasslands are composed of coarse, yellowish mat-grass which thrives on tracts of infertile soils. The lusher, greener areas, however, represent places where so-called basic rocks break down easily to create patches of more nutritious soil.

# 3   The Devil's Kitchen: Idwal

*Introduction*
For anyone interested in the Ice Age this excursion into Cwm Idwal is essential, for it was here, around 1840, that scientists first recognised evidence that glaciers had once been present in Britain. For remarkably little effort you can wander through some of Snowdonia's most spectacular glacial scenery and mingle with rock climbers, botanists and geologists. Because it is such a classic landscape this remarkable glacial hollow is often thronged with visitors and its paths are well marked.

*The walk*
It is not far off the main road but far enough to get very wet in a sudden shower, so take waterproofs. Furthermore, stout footwear is essential, as the

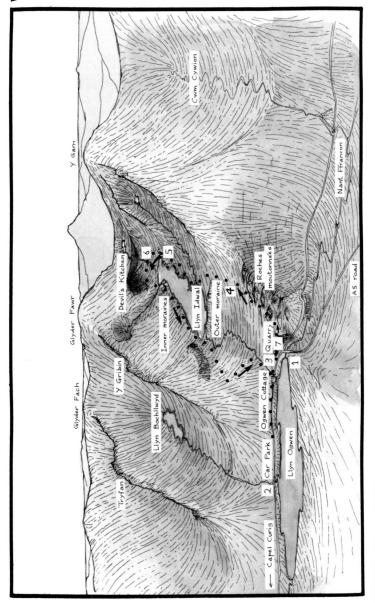

1 ➥From Bethesda A5 south or from Capel Curig A5 west

paths are boggy in places. Allow at least 2 hours to walk round the lake shores and an extra hour if you decide to venture to the top of the Devil's Kitchen. It will be too strenuous for very young children, but older children will cope easily.

*The route*

2 Small 🅿 on by-road at Ogwen Cottage. Large 🅿 about half-way along Llyn Ogwen

At Ogwen Cottage the modern A5 trunk road sweeps majestically through the mountain pass of Nant Ffrancon, as if problematic rock cliffs and waterfalls never existed. But before Telford's engineering feats it was a very different story. Look underneath the road bridge, where the Ogwen river tumbles steeply down from its Llyn Ogwen outlet, and you will see a fragile packhorse bridge precariously spanning the torrent. This was the former crossing-point (near to the former Ogwen mill) where the old route through the pass descended steeply along the line of the present by-road which snakes along its western flank.

3 Cross small Idwal stream and walk up past quarry on left

Ignore the well trodden direct track to Cwm Idwal alongside the outdoor pursuits centre and start off along the by-road, where a vertical gash has been hacked into the hillside. This quarry (in which rock climbers regularly practice) was once the source of so-called hone stones, used extensively for sharpening scythes and other metal blades. The rock was formed hundreds of millions of years ago when volcanic ash, erupted from an ancient volcano, fell into muddy lake waters where it mingled to produce this remarkably hard band of stone.

After having crossed open ground and climbed over a stile in the mountain fence you will have entered the Cwm Idwal Nature Reserve so please respect the vegetation. On the right are some smooth rocky outcrops which not only exhibit the polishing, scratching and grooving of former glaciers but also provide an excellent viewing point for the Nant Ffrancon itself. Look first at the rock surfaces and you will see the long parallel scratches where the basal ice once dragged chisel-like stones across their south-facing (up-valley) sides. These smooth, hard, whale-backed sandstone rocks terminate in north-facing cliffs, however, for the same glaciers and their rocky tools plucked at the down-valley face and slowly prised lumps of it away as they moved down the rock-step. Such was their resemblance to reclining sheep that these smooth rocks were termed '*roches moutonnées*'.

You can now see how this line of ice-scoured crags is part of a massive rock barrier which spans the valley and terminates the gigantic U-shaped trough of Nant Ffrancon. Note how the glacial hollows occur only on the left-hand valley wall – facing north-east for reasons noted on p. 7. Imagine the scene in the Ice Age, when a gigantic glacier moving from right to left along the valley in which Llyn Ogwen lies then descends in a huge icefall into the Nant Ffrancon. Here it is joined by the large tributary glacier from Cwm Idwal, their combined power being sufficient to gouge out the valley bottom below the hard rock band. All is quiet, except for the occasional crash of an avalanche from the surrounding cliffs; there is no bleating of sheep nor roar of waterfalls. Instead of rushy green meadows, and stream-laced hillsides a black and white arctic wilderness of rock, ice and snow prevails.

Now imagine the scene after the glaciers had melted and the streams had returned to the hillsides. The overdeepened rocky basins (cwms) are then filled with sparkling lakes. Of these, Idwal and Ogwen lakes have survived but that which once filled Nant Ffrancon has now disappeared, gradually infilled by gravel and mud brought down from the mountains as the streams have striven manfully to move the mantle of glacial debris. The dark marshy tracts of Nant Ffrancon mark the former lake site. And Llyn Ogwen is quickly infilling too: it is now only about 12 feet (3.6 m) deep. Llyn Idwal, however, is a different matter and that is your next stopping point.

There is no doubt that the great amphitheatre of Cwm Idwal was scoured out by ice, for glaciers have left their mark everywhere. Look first to the head of the lake where the brooding cliffs of the Devil's Kitchen dominate the scene. Here is the backwall of the glacial hollow, steepened by the chiselling and splitting action of alternate freezing and thawing at the interface of rock and ice. The cliffs themselves show layer upon layer of rocks, all gently folded into the shape of an enormous hammock. Most of the layers are composed of ancient lava flows, alternating with thicknesses of hardened volcanic ash, but the topmost rocks are particularly interesting because they have sufficient lime content to support some very rare Alpine plants. These led early botanists to pioneer hair-raising climbs on these dangerous cliffs, but on no account should *you* venture off the track! The vertical cracks in the cliffs have been etched into narrow fissures, the central chasm being worn

4 Note fenced experimental grazing plot on descent to Llyn Idwal

most deeply back by the waterfall of the Devil's Kitchen itself, or Twll Ddu ('the black cleft'). The massive block screes below the cliffs have accumulated periodically since the glaciers departed. One rock fall occurred only a few years ago, but most of them took place when the climate was much colder, some 10 000 years previously.

5 Keep to the path: erosion is severe hereabouts

As you thread your way through the grassy hummocks, which give an uneven shore to the innermost part of the lake, you may wonder if they are the same as the smooth rocky mounds that you encountered earlier on. Instead of being composed of glacially moulded bedrock, however, almost all these hummocks are built from boulders, clay and gravel dumped by the glacier in the form of moraines. Between the hummocks are peaty hollows, created where buried ice blocks slowly stagnated and caused a final collapse of the morainic debris. There are other moraines in Cwm Idwal which show the former limits of the small ice tongue which once existed here. Look back down the lake and you will see a low curving grassy ridge running around its outer end. This was once a frontal moraine, built when the glacier had retreated from the Nant Ffrancon valley but stood at the lip of the cwm itself. The lake which replaced the glacier must once have stood a few feet higher and you can see its former shoreline as a green terrace on the flank of the impounding moraine. As the outlet stream has cut down through the loose glacial material it has gradually lowered the lake level, but now the stream has reached bedrock its rate of wearing down has been slowed considerably and the lake surface remains virtually constant. Now look directly across the lake to the opposite hillside and there above the hummocks you can pick out four parallel lines of lighter coloured grassland running obliquely up the slope. Each marks the position of a marginal moraine formed successively as the glacier slowly melted both downwards and backwards into its hollow.

6 Choice of routes: easy low-level along lake shore; rugged path to foot of waterfall and tricky stream crossing; strenuous route to skyline up left cliffside (and return)

For the majority of walkers it is probably easier to cross the head of the valley by way of the grassy flats near the lake. These flats are part of a delta built out by the Devil's Kitchen stream into the lake. You will also cross a trail of angular, fresh-looking rocks that mark the line of an avalanche/rock fall which occurred only a few years ago. Eventually, you will reach the foot of the smooth rock face known as the Idwal Slabs, here to watch the intrepid rock climbers at play. These steeply

tilted rock layers are one of the lowest bands of rock in the Devil's Kitchen cliffs, and they curve down beneath your feet before reappearing, tilting the other way, on the other side of the amphitheatre. They comprise one of the lowest beds in the Idwal downfold.

As you wend your way slowly back down Cwm Idwal along the well worn track, notice how the tiny island in the lake has a much thicker growth of heather and bilberry than the surrounding shores. This is because sheep have never grazed there, thus allowing these shrubby species to survive. The wire netting plots that you passed earlier are controlled Nature Conservancy experiments to exclude grazing from other parts of the nature reserve, in order to see how quickly its natural vegetation returns to normal.

As you reach the end of the lake, note the grey rock face a few yards to your right. It represents a cliff formed where the smooth pre-glacial hillside was abruptly chopped off short by the Idwal glacier. Since then frost action has caused massive

**SILVER BIRCH**  (80 ft; 25 m)

This graceful tree is both fast growing and short lived. It will tolerate a wide variety of soils and will survive in the most rigorous climates. It is most easily distinguished by its silver-grey scored bark and small toothed leaves. Because of its short life, the silver birch never makes a dominant forest form.

(Opposite) **Hummocky moraines near the head of Llyn Idwal**

slices of the exposed rock to split off from the face; they now lie drunkenly in a chaotic pile at the cliff foot.

7 Keep to path: short cut is boggy

A brisk walk back to Ogwen Cottage Outdoor Pursuits' Centre brings you down to the road again and a welcome cup of tea at the neighbouring snack bar.

# 4   A hanging valley: Cwm Tregalan

Half a day

## Introduction

Perhaps more than any of the other mountain walks the ascent of the Watkin Path into one of Snowdon's largest hollows, encapsulates all that is best in North Welsh scenery. It starts in delightful oakwoods, climbs steadily past a staircase of waterfalls, crosses grassy slopes where Welsh black cattle peacefully graze, before reaching a solitary ice-scraped valley, high on the slopes of Snowdon itself. It is a walk full of interest and with only a relatively gentle gradient on an excellent footpath. Children will find it easy going and will discover the delights of the mountainside without being in any danger. If you try it on a hot, sunny day you will find that the plunge-pools beneath the cataracts have much to offer for aching feet. They also provide excellent swimming and paddling pools. Allow about 2½ hours for the return journey, or longer if you dawdle by the river. As you drive to Bethania, past the wooded lake shores of Nant Gwynant, there are few hints of the dramatic scenery which lies ahead.

## The walk

1 ↬ From Beddgelert A498 east or from Capel Curig A4086 and A498 west. Bethania 🅿 🖉 🅿🄾

The walk starts a short distance from the car park at a cattle grid on the north side of the road where a public footpath sign announces the Watkin Path (opened in 1892). This is one of the traditional routes to Snowdon's summit but since it starts so low down it is also one of the longest: the 3300 feet (1000 m) of ascent will take 4–5 hours. So unless you're feeling very energetic be content with this curtailed walk which includes all the interesting parts and none of the final slog. If you want to reach the summit try Walk 2, because it starts at the same altitude of 1100 feet (335 m) at which this one finishes. Alternatively, take the train.

## The route

The thick oakwoods of Nant Gwynant are a reminder of what Snowdonia's natural vegetation once comprised. Today only a few patches remain,

(Opposite) **Tilted and ice-smoothed rock layers of the Idwal Slabs**

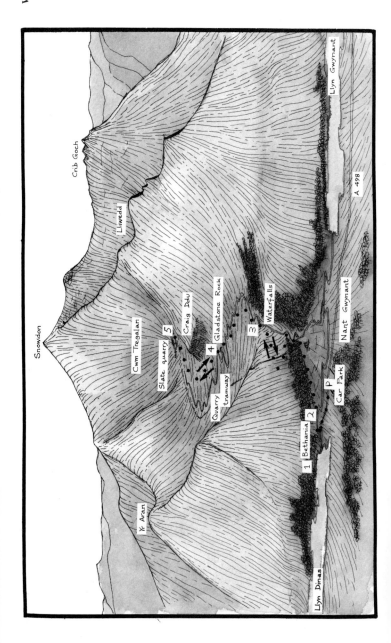

and it is interesting to learn that widespread de-
forestation began as early as the 13th century when
Edward I's armies felled some of the forests which
were giving cover to the opposing Welsh freedom
fighters. Below the woodlands are the flat, stone-
walled fields of the valley floor, occupying the flood
plain of the Afon Glaslyn. The smooth grassland
would not always have appeared so green and
fertile; once it was boggy and littered with stones
dropped by the Glaslyn stream which meandered
across its broad expanse. But local farmers drained
the ground and used the stones to build the field
walls and the farm house which nestles in a
sheltered spot above the flood level and on a
south-facing slope. But if the Glaslyn river merely
burbles past the farmer's front garden, that is
certainly not true of the mountain stream behind
the farm. Here, the slopes steepen, the tributary
stream (which your route follows) races and leaps
down the valley wall and you begin to feel the pull
on your calf muscles as the gradient increases.

The well graded Watkin Path leaves the woodland and follows a broad sweeping arc across
bracken-covered slopes because it was carefully
engineered by 19th-century workmen. The stream,
however, takes the line of least resistance and
plunges from its upland valley down to the floor of
Nant Gwynant in a series of cascades and small
waterfalls. The precipitous rocky step over which it
descends is made of particularly hard volcanic
rocks, tilted into almost vertical layers by ancient
earth movements. Each waterfall is doing its best to
ease the gradient, as each of their plunge pools
shows. Stones carried over the falls and trapped in
the pools swirl round and round grinding away at
the smooth walls of the cauldrons, wearing them
back bit by bit.

The rock cliff on either flank of the waterfalls did
not prove such an obstacle to the path builders nor
to the slate quarrymen, for on the left-hand face
you can see the remains of a quarry incline which
plummets down the slope from the former tramway of the upper valley, but do not follow it. As you
reach the top of the steep section of the path you
will be surprised by the change of scene. Stark,
treeless hillsides, stone-littered moorlands and
bare rocky outcrops greet the eye. What a contrast
from the pastoral landscapes of Nant Gwynant.
Most surprising of all is the nature of the stream
itself. In place of a roaring torrent there is now a
slow, meandering brook because above the rocky

step the upper valley is virtually flat floored again. Because this upper valley is so high above the floor of Nant Gwynant it is called a 'hanging valley' and is one of Snowdonia's best examples.

Look around you and it's not difficult to determine the agent responsible for its form. On the bare rocks by the path you will see the distinctive marks of a former glacier: smoothness on the rocks' up-valley sides, deep scratches running along their sides; on the valley floor itself a filling of glacial debris or 'boulder clay'; at the head of the valley a deep glacial hollow (Cwm Tregalan), from which the glacier was spawned. Here then, during the Ice Age, was a major tributary glacier contributing to the main trunk glacier which once occupied the deeply cut trough of Nant Gwynant. The junction was at the rock step but the difference in height between the respective valley floors was about 1000 feet (300 m), with the tributary valley 'hanging' above the trough. Here the main Gwynant glacier was so much larger than the Tregalan tributary that it was able to cut its valley to a considerably greater depth, leaving the smaller one to descend over the lip by means of an icefall.

3 Just beyond the metal gate

As you continue up the valley the works of nature become subservient to the works of man, for ahead lie the ruins of extractive industries. On the right-hand slope the remnants of copper mining can be seen, matching those of neighbouring Llyn Llydaw on the other side of Lliwedd's mighty precipice (see Walk 2). The white quartz veining in the rocks hereabouts (often mistaken for snow patches) gives a clue to the valuable metal ores which invaded these contorted Snowdonian rocks as subterranean chemical vapours soaked upwards into the crust many millions of years ago. Further on, standing beneath a solitary sycamore, is the skeleton of a slate quarry manager's house, while the abandoned quarry itself is around the next bend in the valley. The South Snowdon quarry, although flourishing in the 1870s, could never compete with its giant competitors at Dinorwig, Bethesda and Blaenau Ffestiniog. Transport costs, by tramway to Nant Gwynant and thence by cart all the way to Porthmadog, were the most serious drawback. In addition, it produced poorer quality slate and there was more waste than usual. The fact that its spoil tips are now largely grass covered suggests that a considerable amount of earth had to be excavated before solid rock was reached and this is unusual in Snowdonia. Thus, the workings

**The Watkin Path to Snowdon at the lip of a hanging valley**

do not look quite as forlorn and disfigured as the massive naked tips of its more important neighbours. A word of warning: do not venture around the workings because some of the pits are very dangerous.

**5** Summit path ascends steeply up right-hand slope

From the quarry Snowdon's summit can be seen, rugged but not very spectacular from this angle. But note the way in which all the slopes surrounding the amphitheatre of Cwm Tregalan soar dramatically upwards for more than 2000 feet (600 m) before culminating in splintered summit ridges. The brooding peaks stand high because they are built largely from layer upon layer of hard lavas and tough volcanic ash, whereas Cwm Tregalan is floored by slate which erodes more easily. You can now begin to see why the ice-scoured hanging valley is so well developed, rimmed on virtually all sides by the resistant volcanics. But just to prove

*Cwm Tregalan* 107

The ice-scoured Gladstone Rock in Cwm Tregalan

that nothing is as simple as it first appears, the shapely pyramid of Yr Aran (2451 feet (747 m)), Snowdon's southwestern foothill, is carved not from volcanics but from slate!

As you turn back down the track, leaving the gaunt quarrymen's barracks, ponder on the activity which once brought smoke and noise to this quiet valley. You will already have seen the 2 ton granite plaque on Gladstone's Rock and read its inscription. It illustrates something of the popularity of this area even a century ago. Presumably, Mr Gladstone was quite unaware that he stood on a glacially scoured rock ('*roche moutonée*'), when he delivered his address. Nor would he have cared that the precipice of Craig Ddu, with its magnificent skirt of buff-coloured screes, that stood foresquare in front of him, belied its name. Craig Ddu means 'black crag' and *that* it certainly is not, for its resistance and colour are due to a thick hard band of yellowish volcanic rock. The Welsh place names are usually so accurately descriptive that this cliff name remains an anomaly, in the same way as the slaty rocks of Yr Aran. Which just goes to prove that neither man nor nature are always perfect.

# 5 Picturesque and sublime: the Betws-y-Coed area

Half a day

## Introduction

The pretty village of Betws-y-Coed is an excellent route centre. It is a sort of Clapham Junction, for its environs mark the meeting place of four river valleys; a junction of the tributary Machno, Lledr and Llugwy rivers with the trunk stream of the Conwy, all within the space of 3 miles (4.8 km). The walk gives you an opportunity to explore sublime gorges and waterfalls, to examine the ways in which rivers mould the landscape, to picnic among the picturesque beauties of their woodland glades and above all to marvel at the ingenuity of the road and bridge builders who have grappled with this difficult terrain.

## The walk

The long walk is relatively easy, partly on metalled roads and partly on woodland paths. It is a walk that will fascinate children but a word of warning, keep a close eye on them when you're following the riverside paths which often become slippery, especially after rain. Allow about 3–4 hours for the long walk, or longer if you picnic or visit the woollen mill or do both. For a shorter walk, follow **1**, **2**, **3**, **4**, **5** and **10** (1–2 hours).

## The route

**1 Betws-y-Coed**
**P wc PO ⌀ ⌷ ☎**
**ℹ M ⌂**

In the centre of Betws-y-Coed is one of Wales' most frequented bridges, Pont-y-Pair ('bridge of the cauldron') named from the turbulent pool created by the Llugwy river as it cascades over its rocky bed. The five-arched stone bridge is possibly of 15th-century construction and you can see how it is firmly anchored on solid rock at either end in order to withstand the ravages of nature. This is more than can be said for the thin veneer of soil which once mantled the river banks, for in a very short span of time visitors have trampled it away, exposing the roots of the trees which now cling precariously to the slaty bedrock.

**2 Follow river-bank path**

Above this important bridging point the valley of the Llugwy widens and the river glides more slowly through the sheltered water meadows. These valley grasslands provide valuable food and shelter for the upland flocks which are brought down from the mountains for the lambing season, but the pastures are often prone to flooding when rainstorms turn these peaceful rivers into raging torrents. The ability of streams to carry debris eroded from the mountainland depends on the

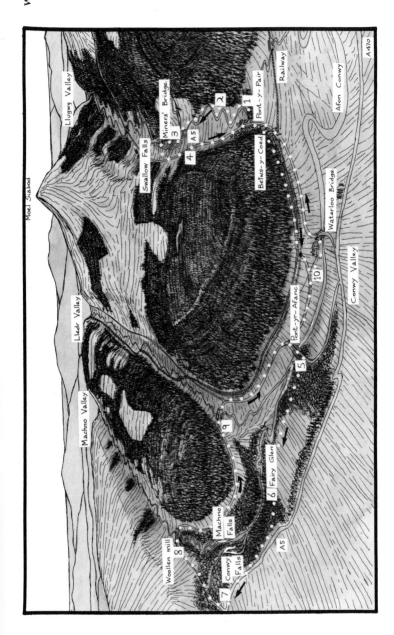

Moel Siabod

Llugwy Valley

Lledr Valley

Machno Valley

Swallow Falls

Miners' Bridge

3

4

A5

2

1

Pont-y-Pair

Betws-y-Coed

Railway

Afon Conwy

Waterloo Bridge

Conwy Valley

A470

10

Pont-yr-Afanc

9

5

Fairy Glen

6

Machno Falls

Woollen mill

8

7

Conwy Falls

A5

velocity and volume of their water, on the steepness of the river channel and on the size of the rocky material which is being moved. If you look in the river bed you will see some very large boulders lying there, around which the current now swirls, apparently incapable of budging them. The largest have probably never moved since they were dumped by glaciers more than 20 000 years ago; the smaller ones may occasionally move a few yards during an exceptional flood; the pebbles, however, will periodically roll and bounce downstream, especially when the river is in winter spate. The smallest debris of all is the mud and silt which is regularly carried within the current itself, discolouring the crystal waters after rain. Remember these variously sized pieces of rock for they are the river's tools, since water alone is virtually incapable of wearing away most of the hard rocks of Snowdonia. Later in the walk you will see their handiwork. About ½ mile (1 km) upstream you can appreciate how in places streams also dump their rocky debris *en masse*, especially where their current slackens as the gradient eases. Here a tiny but steep tributary descends southwards from the wooded plateau and has built out a fan of gravel and boulders onto the valley floor, giving a splendid site for the farmhouse standing sheltered beneath the wooded hillside.

**3** Over ladder stile

Soon after you re-enter the woods the valley narrows again and solid rock once more appears in the river banks. Here is the sloping wooden ramp of the Miners' Bridge, its predecessor once used by 19th-century workers en route from their Pentre Du homes (the village facing you) to the now defunct lead mines on the northern bank (see Drive 1). It is another example of solid rock footings being used by the early bridge builders, and is reputedly sited at the crossing point of a Roman road.

**4** Cross Miners' Bridge, turn left on A5. In Betws-y-Coed turn right on side street 300 yards (300 m) past church. Follow it to Fairy Glen hotel (1 mile, 1.6 km)

Back on the banks of the river Conwy, south of Betws-y-Coed, you will come to a more substantial stone bridge, known as Pont-yr-Afanc ('the beaver's bridge'), named from the deep river pool of Llyn-yr-Afanc on the river Conwy. Although beavers are said to have survived in Welsh rivers until the 12th century, it is likely that they had disappeared in North Wales long before that time. The most notable of the present day wildlife is the salmon which you may see leaping in the neighbouring gorges and cataracts if you are lucky. In summer wagtails and dippers dart among the riverside boulders in this picturesque sylvan

*The Betws-y-Coed area*    111

glade, while evening walkers may glimpse bats flitting through the trees. Here is an idyllic picnic spot, across the river from the Fairy Glen hotel.

5 Follow lane to right of hotel

As you follow the quiet lane uphill beside the hotel you will probably be surprised to learn that this was formerly the main road to London, once characterised by teams of panting horses which would labour to pull a stage coach up the incline from the bridge. The arched stone Pont-yr-Afanc was completed in 1800 just in time to be superseded by Thomas Telford's Waterloo Bridge, which you will see later on. But the roar of tumbling water is more likely to catch your attention, for down to your right is one of Snowdonia's most famous beauty spots – The Fairy Glen.

6 Path to Fairy Glen is through gate opposite wooden hut

Artists and writers of the Romantic Age were always searching for sublime scenery some of which is to be found here: a narrow chasm, flanked by steeply tilted rock walls and bottomed with fang-like rocks; white water tumbling and swirling down the gorge; a canopy of trees meeting overhead as in a great cathedral nave; sunlight filtering through to dapple the mossy rocks and ferns and add sparkle to the waters.

After having admired the spectacle, pause to think about the contrasting nature of the river Conwy hereabouts. At the Beaver's Pool you saw the river ambling along a gently sloping tract, with scarcely any further steepening to disturb its progress to the sea some 16 miles away. In the Fairy Glen, however, the waters are obviously cascading down the last tread of a rocky staircase. In the upper reaches of any river the gradient is bound to be steeper as it leaves the mountainland, but while the railway engineer and the modern road builder can overcome the steepening artificially by constructing ramps and cuttings to maintain a gentle grade, the river has no such luck. But nature is trying hard to smooth out the rock steps in its valleys and this is where the river's tools have come in handy. Its pebbles and cobbles have battered and bludgeoned the river bed with some success ever since the Ice Age terminated. The Fairy Glen was once the site of a large waterfall, but as the pebbles scoured and ground away in the pool at the foot of the fall they have undermined the step and worn it back bit by bit. Over thousands of years the waterfall has moved slowly upstream: you will visit it soon, one mile (1.6 km)

(Opposite) **The Conwy Falls**

**7** Return to old coach road and turn right to join A5. Follow it to Conwy Falls hotel **WC** 🚻. Nature Trail

**8** Leave A5 on B4406 [Penmachno >]. At Woollen Mill (see Appendix) turn right over River Machno

**9** Take right fork at road junction to reach Lledr bridge

**10** Follow A470 to Pont-yr-Afanc but do *not* cross Conwy river. Fork left for Betws-y-Coed and take track on right (500 yards, 500 m beyond Fairy Glen hotel). Pass large hotel near Waterloo Bridge. Last 100 m of path needs restoration (1984)

up the valley, at the spectacular Conwy Falls. In the neighbouring Machno valley you will later pass another waterfall (the Machno Falls) tumbling over a further rock step, slightly higher upstream.

Once you have torn yourself away from the fascinating thunder of the Conwy Falls (and its tempting café) it comes as something of a relief to leave the A5 trunk road and turn into the quieter valley of the Afon Machno. The Penmachno woollen mill is an obvious stopping point not only to sample its wares but also to appreciate its typical siting near a waterfall or cataract in order to make use of the stream power. Just below the mill is the so-called Roman Bridge, a frail, picturesque, mossy arch of cleverly fitted stones. It is in fact an old packhorse bridge, constructed a few centuries ago, probably to service the older but now abandoned Pandy Mill whose shell stands a short distance downstream at the Machno Falls. The process of 'pandying' is one which involved kneading soaps and acids into the newly woven woollen tweeds to close up their fibres.

The by-road meanders northwards between the steep, wooded hillside and the deep Conwy gorge, affording glimpses of the Machno–Conwy river confluence and a different view of the Conwy Falls, before finally leading down to the graceful arch of the Lledr river bridge. Scramble down to the river bank on its upstream side and you will begin to understand how rivers can cut down their rocky beds. Here are a number of smoothly scoured pot-holes, some containing pebbles that are swirled around like grindstones whenever the river is in spate. You can also appreciate how the natural oakwoods have survived mainly along these rocky water courses, while the surrounding hillsides have been recently clothed with exotic conifers.

On the return journey to Betws-y-Coed you will finally be faced by the famous cast-iron Waterloo Bridge built in 1815 and standing resplendent today as another memorial to the magnificent achievements of Thomas Telford. Note how he brought his superbly graded A5 road down the Conwy rock step into Betws-y-Coed and up again into the Llugwy valley and the mountainland by negotiating other rock steps at the Swallow Falls and the Cyfyng Falls, two miles (3.2 km) and four miles (6.4 km) upstream on the Llugwy, respectively.

(Opposite) **An old stone bridge across the Lledr river: large circular 'potholes' have been worn in the river bed**

# 6  The Glaslyn gorge

Half a day

1 Beddgelert 🅿 **wc**
🆘 ⊘ ⊟ ⬛ ♿

## Introduction

Beddgelert stands unobtrusively as a grey-stone hamlet astride one of the two southern portals to the central mountainland (Betws-y-Coed stands at the other). As you turn a bend in the valley it suddenly appears as a huddle of slated houses crouching around a hump-backed bridge. Because it stands at the junction of two rivers, the Colwyn and the Glaslyn, it is a good route centre. Northwards runs the forested Colwyn valley, eastwards the fine glacial trough of Nant Gwynant (see Drive 2). But it is to the south where much of the interest lies, down river at the famous Aberglaslyn Pass.

## The walk

The walk may take 1–2 hours or, if you return via Cwm Bychan, 3–4 hours. Long walk: **1–7**. The longer route involves a steep descent, so very young children should not be taken, unless you are prepared to carry them part of the way. Short walk: follow **1, 2, 3, 4** and return.

## The route

The fields south of the village are very green and flat in this cradle among the hills. By contrast, to left and right, the rugged slopes appear sombre coloured and disconcertingly steep. Ahead of you the southern skyline is a high wooded ridge, looking as it if affords no possible exit, either for road or river, in that direction. As you follow the grassy riverbank towards the ridge, the Glaslyn river seems to move only slowly through the fields, as if reluctant to approach the frowning rocky obstacle. The water frets at the river bank here, dawdles through a natural swimming pool there, depositing mounds of sand and shingle inbetween. Surely the Glaslyn is not capable of moving those monstrous boulders that punctuate this part of its course? Probably not, they were most probably dropped by streams of ice not water. Such tranquillity is an appropriate setting for the neighbouring grave of the legendary Gelert, from which Beddgelert derives its name.

2 Follow signposted path to Gelert's Grave; keep river on left before crossing river bridge

The gliding stream water is responding to the gentle valley gradient as the river crosses the reclaimed tract of a former lake bed. Here, as the

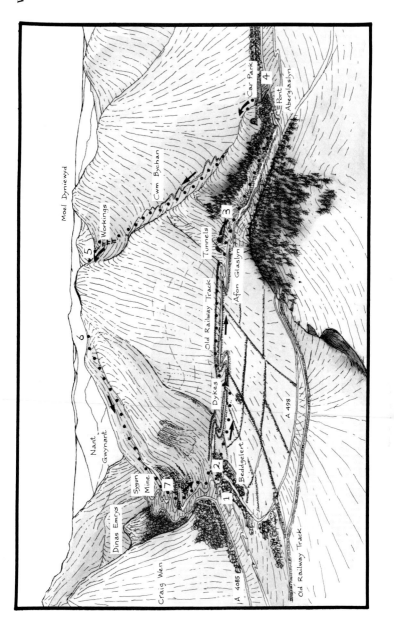

Moel Dyniewyd

Cwm Bychan

Workings

5

Car Park

4

Aberglaslyn

Pont

3

Tunnels

Old Railway Track

Afon Glaslyn

Dykes

A 498

6

Nant Gwynant

7

Sygun Mine

Dinas Emrys

Beddgelert

2

1

Craig Wen

A 4085

Old Railway Track

current slackened, it deposited layer upon layer of mud, sand and gravel for thousands of years until the lake became infilled. But the river is not always in this mood. Sometimes, when swollen by heavy rain it charges down its valley, violent and muddy, over-spilling its banks and turning the sheltered vale back into a lake once more. The artificial embankments (dykes or levees) which follow both banks of the channel are meant to constrain the floodwaters, but are not always successful.

3 After following track through first short tunnel, path descends steeply to river at north end of second tunnel. Pont Aberglaslyn ⚘

You are by now following a similar type of embankment along the left-hand side of the meadowland, but this is not a dyke, only the remains of an abandoned railway track. Perhaps it was another of Wales' tiny mountain railways, once busy with loads of stone, slate or metal ore hacked from the mountain land? But no, this one once carried both goods and passengers between Caernarfon and Porthmadog until it was closed in 1937. What a tourist attraction it would be today!

Tranquillity gives way to clamour as the river plunges into its spectacular gorge. A steep-walled, boulder-strewn, chaotic staircase of leaping white water, hedged in by a frieze of majestic but curiously somnolent pine trees which give the final touch to the alpine scene. How, you ask, did the Glaslyn cut such a gap through this thick layer of very hard volcanic rock? The answer is that it did not, it merely followed a channel carved out under very different circumstances. More than 20000 years ago a valley glacier came this way, escaping southwards from Snowdon and moving out towards the lowlands. En route it encountered this outcrop of obdurate rock that resisted all the grinding of the boulder-armoured sole of the ice and forced the glacier to ride up and over it. But during a later phase the base of the glacier carried a stream of ice meltwater, which moved swiftly downvalley towards its snout along a narrow tunnel beneath the ice. Under tremendous pressure this jet of water used the loose glacial boulders as battering rams to bludgeon relentlessly at the stubborn rock band, thereby fashioning a narrow sub-glacial channel, later to be followed by the infant Glaslyn, as soon as the ice had disappeared.

At Pont Aberglaslyn (Glaslyn Bridge) the river once entered the tidal waters of the Irish Sea but this is no longer true, following the work of William Madocks some 150 years ago (see Drive 3). Imagine how different this spot must once have been when seawater washed the surrounding cliffs

*Walks* 118

The former railway tunnels of the Aberglaslyn gorge are now a riverside path

before exposing yellow sandbanks as the tide receded.

From here you may retrace your steps back to Beddgelert on either bank of the river or, if you are more adventurous, return via Cwm Bychan and the hill tops. The route follows the small stream which drains Cwm Bychan. This narrow, south-facing valley is pleasantly warm on a sunny day but

**4** Follow A4085 [Penrhyndeudraeth >] to **P** where route map is displayed

*The Glaslyn gorge* 119

funnels the prevailing wind in poorer weather. After the tumult of the Glaslyn gorge the tiny, crystal-clear stream of Cwm Bychan comes as something of a relief although the valley's scenery is pretty rather than dramatic. This is due in part to the magnificent oak and chestnut woodland of its lower reaches and the sporadic rowan and birch higher up. Furthermore, a veritable forest of rhododendron (escaped from a Victorian estate in the valley below) is gradually colonising the slopes, encroaching slowly up the hillsides. Such vegetation 'softens' the scene and implies that some soil nutrients must have survived on these otherwise harsh hillslopes. Yet at the head of the Cwm, well above the trees, the gaunt ruins of a copper mine belies such an implication, for when excess copper is flushed into the soil it poisons the vegetation. But the gantries are now broken and rusted, the tips are overgrown and sheep graze quietly in place of the former industrial hubub. It is interesting to learn, nevertheless, that in the 1950s the frenzied activity returned briefly, albeit in a different form. Here was the location of a film – *The Inn of the Sixth Happiness* – because the local landscape resembles that of Northern China.

**5** Above mine workings follow left fork path past small lake

The grassy path climbs to the left-hand skyline past a lonely but attractive pool set amidst rocky knolls. Distant southern views of the sea at Porthmadog and the sweeping coastal hills at Harlech make the gentle climb up Cwm Bychan worthwhile. The gap on the ridge, however, reveals a more spectacular view north-eastwards across Nant Gwynant to the towering ridges of Snowdon (see Walks 2 and 4). As you scramble down the mountainside, you finally descend to the ruined Sygun copper mine, standing forlornly amidst a riot of rhododendrons, like some jungle-swamped Mayan temple. The route follows a road and then a riverside path back to Beddgelert, passing the prominent wooded hill of Dinas Emrys which rises steeply from the valley floor on the far bank of the river. Its rocky cone is one of Wales' most famous hillforts, which was first occupied by Iron Age settlers, then possibly used as a defensive site by the Romans before being strongly fortified by the Norman invaders.

**6** Pass cairn and go through gap in ridge-top wall. Path descends steeply to Sygun mine

**7** At mine turn left and keep on riverside road, then path, back to Beddgelert

(Opposite) **The Aberglaslyn gorge**

Derelict machinery from the former copper mine of Cwm Bychan

# 7  Vortigern's valley and Yr Eifl peaks

Half a day *or* full day

## Introduction

**1** ⬆ From Caernarfon A499 south and B4417 at Llanaelhaearn, or from Pwllheli A499 north and B4417

The walks in this area make a change from the inland valleys and high peaks, for the isolated Yr Eifl massif is dominated by the sea which pervades the view at every turn of the path. Yr Eifl (popularly known as The Rivals) is the westernmost peak of Snowdonia, its last defiant rampart before completely surrendering to the Irish Sea. It is a breezy and airy place where you can either wander freely uphill over heathery slopes, visiting the magnificent Iron Age hillfort of Tre'r Ceiri (**6** (6)) or gaze down into the working stone quarries of its northern face (**3** (3)). One of the most fascinating walks, however, goes downslope from the car park, not up.

## The walk

Allow at least half an hour to reach Porth-y-Nant, and double that time if you decide to go all the way to the beach to picnic or bathe. Note that the road down to Porth-y-Nant is not fit for anything but a Land Rover, so leave your car behind. It is a very steep ascent on the return, so remember that tired toddlers may have to be carried! Long walks can include **3** (1½ hours) and **6** (1 hour). Short walk: follow **2, 4, 5** and return (1–2 hours).

## The route

**2** 🅿 reached by turning uphill from B4417 [Nefyn >] road at Llithfaen post office

From the car park the conical peak of Yr Eifl ('a trident') dominates the scene. It looks remarkably like a volcanic cone and you'd be forgiven if you presumed it to be an extinct Vesuvius, particularly if you'd heard that it was composed of rocks created in the fiery bowels of the Earth. The truth is rather different, however, so it is no use toiling to its summit expecting to find a crater, as some of your forefathers did. Between 400 million and 500 million years ago volcanoes *were* present in Snowdonia (see p. 5), ejecting lavas and ashes which have subsequently become hardened into the rocks which build many of the highest peaks. All semblance of those erstwhile conical vents has long since been destroyed by downwearing of the land surface, but the same eroding agencies have also exposed several of the deep chambers which once supplied the volcanic lava. Because the molten material was at such depth beneath the crust it

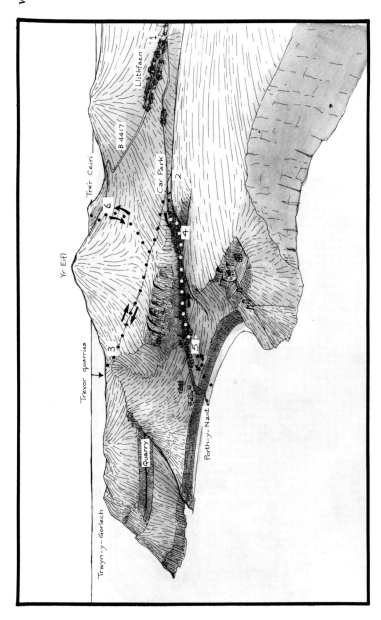

Trwyn-y-Gorlech

Yr Eifl

Trevor quarries

Tref Ceiri

Quarry

Porth-y-Nant

Car Park

Llithfaen

B 4417

1

2

3

4

5

6

cooled slowly, giving time for large rock crystals to form. Long after these deep-seated rock masses, such as granite, became uncovered, they have frequently been quarried not only for their beautifully coloured building stone but more often because of their considerable durability. The Yr Eifl stone quarries at Trevor produce a grey granite which, after crushing, is used extensively for road surfacing throughout Britain. You have probably driven over some of it on your journey to North Wales.

3 You can walk (40 mins return) or drive uphill from **P** to look down into Trevor stone quarries

As you begin to descend the steep track into the isolated valley of Nant Gwrtheyrn a spruce forest quickly veils the view. Nevertheless, you may wonder how this puzzling blind valley came into being for it is very different from anything you have seen so far. It is so deep, so short and occupied by such a minor stream, trickling along its floor, that you may even think that it was man made, especially when you see the abandoned quarry faces all around. It seems unlikely that the tiny stream could ever have been capable of carving out this curious amphitheatre. But there are a few clues if you look carefully. As you pick your way down towards the hairpin bends look at the natural road surface beneath your feet (where it has not been reinforced by odd patches of concrete). The bare rock exposures are made of black shaly slate which crumbles easily under your heel and it is this rock which underlies the valley itself. At the second hairpin bend where the road again doubles back on itself a small footpath continues straight on towards the sea. Follow it until you emerge from the trees on to a steep, boulder-covered slope. These massive stone blocks are light grey in colour and have clearly fallen from the cliffs above. They will not crumble beneath the heel of your boot, not surprisingly, for these are tough, granite-like rocks which build the walls and peaks of this natural amphitheatre, later to be sporadically blasted and hewn by quarrymen. It is, therefore, the differences in rock hardness which partly explains the valley depth. One rock has been easier for nature to wear down than has the other.

4 Short walk off road to view blocky screes

Return to the road, for the path down across the screes is both tedious and dangerous because the boulders are often slippery, especially after rain. Near the bottom of the zig-zags you will have opportunities to look back at the valley head and a surprise awaits you, for the relatively gentle lower slope of Yr Eifl (near the car park) has suddenly

*Vortigern's valley and Yr Eifl* 125

turned into a vertical cliff. If it were nearer to the sea you would easily mistake it for a sea cliff but you may have seen these precipitous rock faces before, perhaps in Cwm Idwal (see Walk 3). Thus, you'd be right in thinking that this must be the backwall of a glacially eroded hollow or 'cwm'. A tiny glacier, first nourished by snowdrifts on Yr Eifl, once chiselled out this depression by taking advantage of the more easily eroded slates. Two other cwms occur on Yr Eifl's north-facing slopes, alongside the gigantic quarries.

A further surprise, as you emerge from the woodland, is the lonely, partly ruined village standing fore-square on its ledge above the sea. Attempts are being made to renovate some of its buildings, mainly by voluntary labour, for the weather has already destroyed many of the old roofs since this quarry village was abandoned. Choirs no longer sing in its empty chapel. Its glassless windows stare blindly out. Altogether a ghostly atmosphere on a sunless or misty day, so it is hardly surprising that the hidden valley has evoked legends. It is said that the 5th-century British King Vortigern died here in exile, exhausted after the unsuccessful defence of his kingdom against marauding bands of Picts and Scots.

5 Opened in 1983 by HRH The Prince of Wales as a Welsh Language Study Centre

If you choose to descend further, past the ruined crushing plant, the secluded shingle beach is quickly reached. It is littered with rusting machinery and the remains of a pier from which the stone was once shipped. Sea transport was both cheaper and more convenient when demand was heavy, but as post-war reconstruction of British cities was largely completed and granite was replaced by other types of building materials so its requirement dwindled. Smaller inland quarries could now send the stone by road, so that many of these peripheral Welsh quarries were closed, leaving a forlorn but nevertheless fascinating record in the landscape.

6 Allow 90 mins walk to Tre'r Ceiri (rough ground, poor paths). Cut across hillside to right of Yr Eifl summit and Tre'r Ceiri hill will come into view

A walk to visit the well preserved hill fortress of Tre'r Ceiri would be a worthwhile exercise for the energetic, either as an alternative to descending Nant Gwrtheyrn, or better still, as an additional stroll after a picnic lunch. The airy mountain fortress, built on this wonderful vantage point before the Romans came, housed a substantial

(Opposite) **Blocky screes and abandoned stone quarries above Porth-y-Nant**

population during times of tribal stress. Its function was similar to that of the fortress built on Conwy Mountain (see Walk 8) at the other end of the range. It was made easier to construct because Yr Eifl's peaks are littered with frost-shattered rocks and, in one sense, Tre'r Ceiri must have been one of Britain's earliest granite-built 'towns'. Today, like neighbouring Vortigern's valley, its lonely, deserted ruins conjure up legends of the heroic past.

# 8   Village in the clouds: Conwy Mountain

Half a day

## Introduction

**1** ↣ From Conwy, west on Sychnant Pass road or from Penmaenmawr, east on Conwy Old Road

A walk along the ridges of Snowdonia's north-easternmost ramparts provides both far-reaching vistas and a kaleidoscope of colour rarely seen in these khaki uplands. A tapestry of heather and gorse drapes the buff-coloured cliffs while cloud shadows mottle both the coastal hills and the shifting sand dunes at their feet. Beyond all is the glittering backdrop of the Irish Sea. This is a remarkably dry walk, unlike the soggy tracks of the higher mountain land. You are now in the 'rain shadow' of the main mountain mass (see p. 19) but the relative dryness is due partly to the windiness of this exposed corner. So be warned and take a sweater, even on a sunny day.

## The walk

It's not a very strenuous excursion, so older children should cope easily and, with luck, you may see mountain ponies in the first few miles. Allow 3–4 hours for the longest walk (**2–8**). Shorter walks can be made by following **2, 3, 4, 5** and **6** (1–2 hours) or **6, 7** and **8** (1–2 hours).

## The route

**2** 🅿 at highest point of Pass. If full park at roadside towards Conwy. Route is through metal gate opposite 🅿

As soon as you pass the national park boundary signs the landscape changes from hedged and cultivated fields to stone-walled enclosures speckled with bracken and gorse. Here, the sharp break between lowland and upland is a mere 400 feet (122 m) above sea level, where the less resistant mudstones of the Conwy valley give way to the more durable volcanic rocks of Snowdonia. It also marks the zone where the valley's natural

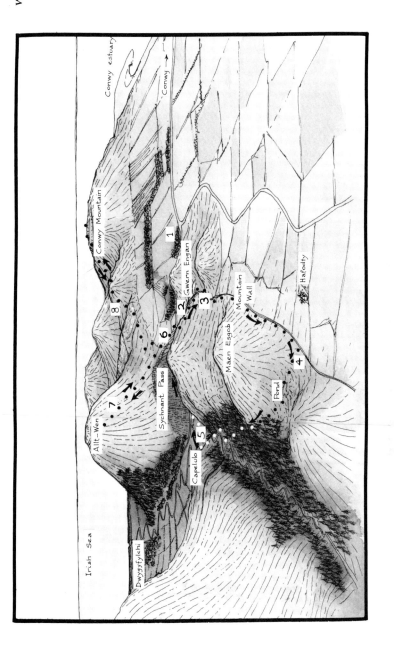

Irish Sea

Conwy estuary

Conwy →

Conwy Mountain

Gwern Engan

Maen Esgob Mountain

Wall

Hafodty

Pond

Allt-Wen

Sychnant Pass

Capelulo

Dwygyfylchi

1
2
3
4
5
6
7
8

woodlands dwindle away into scrub and heathery moorland partly because of the poorer soils. But the hills were not always devoid of trees because the small marshy pool alongside the track was once an alder-fringed swamp, for that is the meaning of its name, Gwern Engan. It was prehistoric man who probably cleared this natural woodland by means of his rudimentary metal, or possibly stone, tools, perhaps from the neighbouring 'axe factory' of Penmaenmawr. He needed the timber for fuel and for roofing his primitive stone huts. A century ago archaeologists excavated a group of hut circles in this tiny valley, the settlement having been located by proximity to a source of water in this relatively streamless environment. Stone Age man was forced to dwell on the hill tops before he was able to clear the thick woodlands of the marshy vale, but if you wonder how he survived remember that the climate was much milder than at present. You will see a reasonably well preserved example of a primeval hill village later on your walk.

**3** Follow path uphill to high stone wall on left and keep it on your left

At the crest of the ridge the grassy track strikes off southwards along the line of the mountain wall, itself a monument to the efforts of later Welsh farmers to wring a living from these inhospitable uplands. During the 18th and 19th centuries the prosperous farms on the more fertile soils of the lower slopes had become fragmented by the traditional splitting of the inheritance among the male offspring. The first-born sons had the better plots, forcing the remainder to carve out their livelihood from the less hospitable stony upland slopes. Thus, the high-level summer shelter, formerly occupied only by cattle herders for a few months each year, became a permanent mountain farm (termed a 'shieling' in Scotland and a 'hafod' in Wales). In a fold of the hills, a few hundred yards below the mountain wall, just above a patch of woodland you can see the roof of such a farm, aptly named Hafodty.

**4** Turn right at conspicuous ladder stile in mountain wall. Pass pond and farm before following track down to Capelulo

After having crossed westwards over the brow of the ridge you will be confronted by a deep, wooded gorge. Its tumbling stream (the Afon Gyrach), plunging down this shaded valley, once turned a waterwheel at Capelulo mill. It seems quite natural to accept that the stream waters carved out this deep ravine below you, but how, then, do you explain the gorge which bites deeply into the hillside a mile to the north? This is the famous Sychnant Pass through which the old Conwy–Bangor road threads its tortuous way. Its name is an apt description of this parched chasm ('dry gorge'). The valleyside crags give way to skirts of broken rock which sweep down to its empty floor. But there is not a drop of water to be seen. It's the same shape as the Capelulo valley just round the corner so why hasn't it a stream? If you come from a home in the chalklands or from the limestone tracts of Britain you may think that the stream which once carved it has gone underground, through rocks which will not hold water, or that it runs only seasonally at the surface, like a downland 'bourne'. But you would be wrong. The surrounding rocks are not chalk or limestone and the Sychnant Pass is not a miniature Cheddar Gorge. Could it, therefore, have been gouged out by a glacier? Wrong again, because it has not got the characteristic U-shaped profile of a glacial trough. But you are getting closer to the truth, for the valley was carved by a stream of glacial meltwater escaping westwards from the edge of the thick Welsh glacier which once filled the Conwy valley to its brim. After the ice had melted and its meltstream gone the valley was left high and dry.

5 Turn right and walk up road to top of Pass

The route strikes off northwards at the valley head, beneath a line of remarkable yellowish-coloured cliffs. If you look closely at any of the bare rock faces hereabouts you will find that they look as if the rocks are bedded, i.e. occur in layers. They are not hardened clays or sands, however, but ancient lavas that flowed out of Snowdonia's volcanoes 500 million years ago. Geologists call these particular rocks 'rhyolites', from a Greek word meaning 'to flow', referring to the banding or flow structures formed when the lava poured out under molten conditions. Unlike the dark-coloured lava flows of basalt, which has a high proportion of iron minerals, rhyolite has a chemical composition rich in light-coloured quartz minerals and virtually devoid of iron. Where hot chemical solutions later penetrated the rocks from below (see p. 93) they cooled and crystallised, like in a school-bench chemistry experiment, to give veins of white quartz. Their snowy tracery riddles the western cliffs of the sharp peak of Allt Wen (829 feet (253 m)) to give it its distinctive name ('white cliff').

6 At **P** turn left and follow track

If you are feeling energetic you may like to scramble to the fortified summit of Allt Wen, which was once used by early man as a defensive outpost commanding the narrow defile of the Sychnant Pass. The main fortified settlement of these coastal hills, however, was Castell Caer Leion which

7 Well trodden path to Allt Wen summit

*Conwy Mountain* 131

Rocky cliffs formed from ancient lavas, with Allt Wen beyond

occupies the neighbouring summit of Conwy Mountain (809 feet (246 m)).

**8** Follow any of tracks which ascend Conwy Mountain

You can approach it by any one of a network of paths which criss-cross the sheltered valley between these two rocky peaks. Note how the small farm, huddled amidst its patchwork of emerald-coloured fields, is located by a tiny pool, like an oasis in the wilderness. But there the analogy ceases, for in the late summer months these moorland slopes are ablaze with purple and gold as the heather and gorse weave an unforgettable magic carpet. If you're lucky you will see ravens and possibly kestrels gliding gently on the coastal updraughts. Down on the northern cliffs the very rare chough, a red-legged crow, has nested, but do not go scrambling down in an attempt to see it for the chances are that you will not and the cliffs are very loose and dangerous!

It soon becomes clear why the summit ridge of Conwy Mountain was converted into a hill fort by the so-called Iron Age tribes who settled here long before the Roman invasion. The summit commands views in all directions, especially eastwards to the Conwy estuary; its northern slopes are protected by cliffs; the summit rocks could easily be quarried to build the ramparts (much as the northern slopes were later to be similarly plundered on a larger scale by 19th-century quarrymen).

A profitable half-hour may be spent exploring the remains of this former strongpoint. Imagine what it must have been like living 2500 years ago in this early penthouse: then its broken ramparts would have been much higher; 50 circular huts would have clustered in the centre (probably supporting a population of some 150 souls); the men would have ranged the slopes tending the cattle and sheep; the women would have ground the corn grown in those verdant fields you passed en route (smooth stone grinding slabs, termed 'saddle querns', have been found in the ruins); sentinels would have patrolled the surrounding hill tops, ready to sound a warning of possible attack; the children may have been water carriers, for water supply would have been a constant problem on this breezy hill summit. If you are here on a sunny summer day you will find that other visitors will help recapture the sense of overcrowding. But come here out of season, on a grey day, and it is a lonely place, inhabited only by the birds and ghosts of long-dead warriors. After the Romans had gone, in times of attack, the settlers returned occasionally to take refuge on the hill tops, but their permanent homes were at lower elevations, partly because of the deteriorating climate and partly because of the final clearance of the valley woods and marshes. You can see the walled medieval town of Conwy at your feet; in reality the citadel has merely moved downhill. If you look down the northern slopes you will find that modern man has created a new type of settlement. On Conwy Morfa behind the sand dunes, geometric streets of white caravans echo the greystone chessboard plan of Conwy's castle town (see Walk 11).

# Wet days

## 9   The silver skein: Aber Falls

Half a day

### Introduction

*From Conwy, A55 west or from Bangor, A55 east*

If you are staying on the northern coast, it is pouring with rain and the cloud base is low on the mountains, you can choose between an historic town walk (see Walk 11) or an exhilarating stroll to visit Rhaeadr Fawr ('the big waterfall'), one of Wales' most spectacular waterfalls. It is always preferable to look at waterfalls during or after rain because then they are in spate. In addition, it will give you a chance to polish up on your natural history for the route also follows an interesting nature trail in Coedydd Aber National Nature Reserve, set up by the Nature Conservancy in 1975. The walk will be wet and slippery underfoot so wear boots or stout shoes if it is raining. Plimsolls are dangerous on the wet rocks near the falls! If you visit in dry weather, however, almost any sensible footwear will suffice.

### The walk

Allow about 2 hours for the return journey (**3**, **4** and **5**) which is not strenuous enough to deter grandma or even toddlers. (Note that if you return by the forest section of the nature trail (**3**, **4**, **5** and **6**) it involves a steeper climb so add another hour.)

### The route

1 Aber 🅿 ⌀ 🚻. Turn off A55 and bear right in village

As you turn off the busy coast road (A55) you will appreciate the reasons why the tiny village of Aber was located here. Its name means River Mouth and the first settlement was built around an 11th-century Norman earthwork (Pen-y-Mwd) at the point where the Afon Aber leaves the mountain-land prior to entering the sea. Its gorge is the only real break in the 12 mile (19 km) long northern wall of Snowdonia between the valleys of the Conwy and the Nant Ffrancon. The Romans certainly had an eye for country and brought their road down this coastal cleft from its high mountain pass of Bwlch-y-Ddeufaen (see Drive 1). At the car park the graceful stone bridge of Bont Newydd ('new

(Opposite) **Conwy from Conwy Mountain**

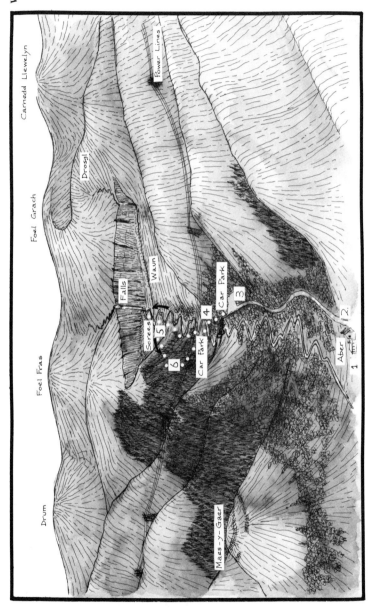

Carnedd Llewelyn

Foel Grach

Drosgl

Foel Fras

Drum

Power Lines

Falls

Waun

Scree

Car Park

Car Park

Maes-y-Gaer

Aber

bridge') stands at the point where the Roman road crossed the river, now marked by the stepping stones below the bridge, although these may well be replacements, put there to assist pack horses in the Middle Ages.

As you set off through the dark woodland glade it is interesting to think that this canopy of oak, ash, hazel and alder must have changed very little since Roman times for this nature reserve incorporates one of the few surviving patches of Snow-donia's primeval forests. In the damp woodland, mosses, lichens and ferns abound, many of them growing on the trees themselves, a sure sign of a wet climate. Look out also for nuthatches, tree creepers and especially for green and great spotted woodpeckers. It is not long, however, before you are jolted back to the present, for modern technology makes its impact in the form of the high voltage electricity cables which leap across the valley, taking power from North Wales' nuclear power stations and hydro-electric schemes to England's voracious cities. Thank goodness that the Aber Falls have not been harnessed!

On leaving the first patch of woodland the higher mountains at last come into view, though the summits are probably shrouded and their slopes festooned with trailing mists. But these mountain slopes are terminated abruptly by a line of precipitous cliffs fronted by vast aprons of shattered stones (screes). The precipice marks the edge of an outcrop of granite-like rock, termed 'granophyre', which cooled slowly from a molten mass deep within the Earth's crust many millions of years ago. During the Ice Age a glacier would have lumbered slowly down this valley, but its legacy is relatively scanty, for of all the larger Snowdonian valleys the Aber gorge is one that is not truly U-shaped, nor are there obvious glacially smoothed rocks to be seen. Instead, frost-action played a more important role in fashioning the scenery hereabouts. Repeated freezing and thaw-ing of the cliffs caused the crags to disintegrate, with the rocky debris constantly contributing to the impressive apron of stones below. You can see how in places these masses of loose stones have become stabilised by vegetation, suggesting that frost action is now considerably less effective than during the arctic climate of some 10 000 years ago. Only near to the waterfall, where visitors have indulged in the dangerous practice of 'scree-running', has the loose debris remained

*Aber Falls* 137

**The head of the Aber valley with screes (left) and waterfall**

unstable because the binding vegetation has been destroyed.

Have you noticed the other vegetation differences in this upper part of the valley? High on the valley sides the Forestry Commission have introduced conifer plantations which flourish on the better drained but poorer, stonier soils. Along the track itself are rushy patches marking the poorly drained, boggy soils, while on the richer soils stretching down to the river below the path is a thick alder woodland (Wern goch), fed by valley-side springs. Alder was once the most typical vegetation of Snowdonia's marshy valley floors, but modern farming has cleared most of their thickets and drained their waterlogged soils. Since this area became a nature reserve the farms have disappeared and the sheep introduced mainly for a grazing experiment on this unpopulated 'wilderness'. Because sheep inhibit the regeneration of young saplings they have been excluded from most of the woodlands hereabouts, except in the area known as the Waun on the opposite valleyside where hummocky boulder clay mantles the ground to the west of the main waterfall. Thus this tract remains an almost treeless grazing area. You can see the boulder clay exposure where it has been cliffed by the river just below the falls.

It may be surprising to learn that this sheltered valley housed a substantial population, some 2000 years ago, in Romano-British times. These early settlers would have made small clearings in the natural woodland to make room for their crops and livestock on the more nutritious soils of the valley floor. In times of attack, perhaps from the sea, they would have climbed to the hill fort of Maes-y-Gaer which overlooks the valley near to Aber village.

Waterfalls come in all shapes and sizes: some are broad, some are narrow, some are high, some are low, some are nothing more than a series of cataracts, others comprise a single vertical leap. The Aber Falls are a narrow, double leap of 117 feet, with the intertwined threads of water looking like a silver skein against the darker rock face. Where the pool has undermined the cliff, huge blocks have peeled off and crashed into a chaotic litter at the foot of the falls. The river is working hard to get rid of this gigantic step in its course but the rock remains obdurate. For thousands of years the gorge has been cut back through the less resistant shales and slates of the lower valley but now the retreat has been held on this harder rock and further cutting back will be painfully slow. In summer you may see grey wagtails or even dippers darting around the stream channel while ravens flap busily overhead. If you are really lucky a buzzard may soar lazily into view above the cliffs as it searches for its prey.

5 If you choose longer upland route (6) return to gate, turn right over ladder-stile. Follow blue-topped posts into woodland

You now have a choice of return routes: back along the original track or diagonally upwards across the steeper hillside, the latter route being the continuation of the nature trail. If you follow the upland route through the woodland notice how two different types of conifer have been planted:

*Aber Falls*   139

lower down on the slopes where grass and bracken once flourished Sitka spruce (the traditional Christmas tree) has been introduced, while on the thinner, stonier soils higher up, lodgepole pine is more appropriate on the poorer heather and bilberry moor. Soon after beginning the gradual descent (by turning left at the junction of the paths) you will enter a clearing in which the remains of a Bronze Age cairn can be found on your left. Some 3500 years ago an important leader must have been buried here within the circle of stones. The cairn has been badly mutilated by weather and by grave robbers intent on recovering the burial ornaments. But it serves to remind you that in those far-off times, before metal tools were widespread, many settlements would have been located on these upland slopes because the valleys would have been too thickly wooded for clearance to be easy. Only when iron tools had become more common, one thousand years later, would the hill farmers have been able to move down the slopes and carve out clearings in the more sheltered valleys. Don't forget that between 500 BC and AD 500 the climate also became more severe and that the hill settlements (such as Maes-y-Gaer hillfort which you can now see on the bare hilltop ahead) were too exposed for continuous occupation. Thus, there is a record of slow abandonment of the higher mountainland and a shift of population to the lowlands where it still remains, leaving the uplands to sheep, moorland birds and occasional walkers like yourselves.

6 Bear left at path junction (do *not* follow blue markers from here on). Leave wood by stile and return to Forestry Commission **P** and thence to Bont Newydd

## 10 Beside the sea: Criccieth beach

Half a day

*Introduction*
Sunny days will probably lure you to Snowdonia's attractive coastlines, but there are some beaches which may be worth a visit even on a wet day. Heavy rainfall and thick cloud cover are not uncommon in Welsh mountainlands so the chances are that one day you will find the Snowdonian heartland so mist shrouded that you will seek out an alternative area to stretch your legs. Where better than the long curving beach at Criccieth which is an exhilarating place to be when a

(Opposite) **The Aber Falls tumbling down a hard granitic rock face**

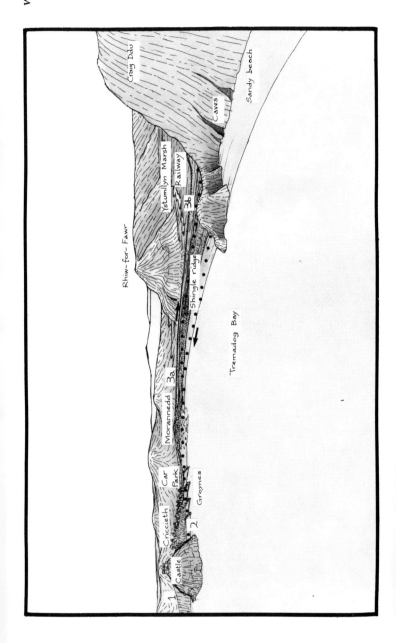

Crag Ddu

Caves

Sandy beach

Rhiw-for-Fawr

Ystumllyn Marsh

Railway

3b

Shingle ridge

Tremadog Bay

Moranedd

3a

Criccieth

Car Park

Groynes

Castle

1

2

**1** Criccieth 🅿 **wc** 🅿️
🚻 🍴 ♿ 📷 . Early
closing Wednesday

southwesterly gale is blowing. Just so long as you have good waterproof footwear and clothing the walk can be very rewarding and you will certainly see the elemental forces of nature hard at work. Furthermore, the rainfall is actually an advantage for the wetter the beach pebbles the more brilliant are their colours. You may even be tempted to bring some home with you so take along a plastic carrier bag just in case.

### The walk

A brisk walk to Black Rock headland will take at least half-an-hour but you can easily double this time if you dawdle, so allow up to 2 hours for the return journey (**1**, **2** and **3**), especially if you want to study the wonderful birdlife that abounds in the Ystumllyn Marsh (**3b**).

### The route

**2** Park at castle end
of sea-front 🅿 and
examine castle rock
and beach defences
first

Before you leave the car park look first at the location of the castle high on the rocky headland. Built originally by Llywelyn the Great, the famous Welsh prince, it was later captured by the invading English armies and rebuilt into its present Anglo-Norman style as one of the ring of Edwardian castles surrounding Snowdonia (see also View 3 and Walk 11). These early builders knew what they were doing for they sited the castle on hard rock, unlike the more modern builders in Criccieth some of whose structures now perch precariously on the edge of rapidly eroding cliffs. Note how extensive artificial cliff-protection works now line the fore-shore between the car park and the castle rock for here the cliffs are made not of solid rock but of much less resistant boulder clay. The authorities acted just in time, before houses fell into the sea.

As you walk back along the beach you will see how the cliff defences soon terminate and where, at Morannedd, the undefended cliff comes under periodic wave attack. Here you will have to pick your way through a scatter of large boulders embedded in the beach. They are of different shapes, colours and textures and are so massive that even the strongest waves find it impossible to move them. It is easy to see that these blocks have fallen from the cliff face and have remained where they fell even though wave attack has driven the boulder clay cliff remorselessly inland year after year. The softer sands and clays which surround those boulders still surviving in the present cliff prove to be very feeble when bludgeoned by a

*Criccieth beach* 143

storm wave and you can see piles of slumped material at intervals at the foot of the slope, where undercutting has caused the face to collapse. If the large boulders remain behind where does the gravel, sand and mud go to? Some of it is combed out to sea by the backwash of the waves but most of it is moved eastwards along the beach, also by wave action.

If you are walking along with a westerly wind at your back you will note how the waves are breaking obliquely across the slope of the beach, pushing sand and shingle ahead of them. But watch what happens as the wave floods back down the beach; it flows back directly not obliquely down the slope because of the law of gravity. Thus, pebbles and sand grains will tend to make a zig-zag journey in the direction which you are walking, but not at the same speed, of course. This is not the entire story, however, for even without a gale, waves must approach this beach from a dominantly southwesterly direction because that is where the open ocean lies; the shape of the land dictates that waves cannot approach from the north and east. You may ask why the movement of beach material is always from west to east on this coastal stretch, because surely the occasional southeasterly wave would send the beach material in the opposite direction? The simple answer is that winds rarely blow from that direction and in any case the prominent headland of Black Rock effectively cuts off any supply of sand and shingle from the east. In fact it acts as an enormous natural breakwater, stopping the easterly movement of the Criccieth shingle just as surely as the artificial wooden breakwaters (groynes) restrict its eastward movement on the town beach itself. These groynes will become increasingly important as time goes on because they will stop the Criccieth town beach from dwindling away and possibly disappearing. Ever since the cliff-foot defence works were completed in the 1960s, in order to protect the cliff-top houses, erosion of the town's boulder clay cliff has been checked just to the east of the castle headland. Thus, the supply of material to create the beach has been seriously depleted and will, in future, come only from offshore, although in considerably smaller quantities. It is the sort of problem that faces most coastal authorities in

(Opposite) **Criccieth beach showing the wave-cliffed (where waves cut a headland into a cliff) glacial clay headland of Morannedd and its boulder-littered foreshore**

resorts built on unstable, crumbling cliffs: a choice between losing property or the beach!

As you walk along the beach notice how it is divided into a seaward stretch of sand (covered at high tide) and a gently curving shingle ridge on the landward side. Waves have pushed the pebbles up the beach to build this ridge and only occasionally will storm waves overtop it, flinging even large pebbles and all sorts of flotsam over onto its inner side. If you climb up to the crest and look across the railway track on the landward side you will discover a featureless marshland infilling a broad hollow between the headland of Rhiw-for-Fawr and Black Rock headland. Although there is now very little open water this marsh is still termed 'Ystumllyn', a brackish lake formed when the coastal bay was cut off from the open sea by the slow eastward extension of the beach ridge on which you are standing. Today it is a place of reeds, rushes and small copses of willow, where coots and grebes dispute their territorial rights with reed buntings, warblers, oyster catchers, lapwings and many other species. It also boasts a colony of black-backed gulls, so bird watchers will find it especially exciting. If you are lucky you may also see otters in the artificial drains. Over the centuries the lake has gradually been infilled by silting and today improved meadowland is gradually replacing its fascinating marshy wilderness. If you happen to be here on a fine day there are many pleasant strolls along the marshland footpaths but it is rather a depressing, squelchy walk in the rain.

Eventually you will reach the rocky headland of Black Rock (Craig Ddu) where the shingle ridge terminates abruptly. You will be surprised to see the sudden fall in the level of the beach beyond the rocky outcrop: too high to climb down to the other side and too dangerous to wade round the point even at low tide. If you must visit the tempting sandy beach of Morfa Bychan on the far side, be sure to follow the cliff path higher up; and even this may be slippery in the rain, so be careful! On the eastern side of the rocky headland the sea has picked out weaknesses to form caves, but for those who resist the temptation to continue, there remains the pleasure of searching the wet shingle to find the most beautiful of the countless numbers of beach pebbles. They create a kaleidoscope of rich colours, sparkling in the rain, ranging from jet black through brilliant reds, oranges, pinks and browns, to dove greys, purples, mauves and pris-

**3** Two official crossings of railway line to reach marsh: one just to the east of Morannedd cliff (**3a**), other at Black Rock Halt (**3b**). Footpaths are not clearly marked

tine whites. Some exhibit miniature folds and dislocations, others remarkably developed banding; some have curious shapes, others are perfectly rounded: all are fascinating.

Pause to think where they have come from. They are obviously quite unlike the solid rock hereabouts so they must have been derived from the boulder clay cliffs at Criccieth more than one mile away. And since the boulder clay is itself made up of rock fragments brought by glaciers from the mountain land, you are handling pieces of rock from all over western Snowdonia. Just think that one of the pebbles in your hand may have started its journey on Snowdon itself, first carried as an angular chunk of rock by a mountain glacier. Its passage down Nant Gwynant and along the lower Glaslyn valley would have rounded its corners and made it smaller as it ground its way slowly over the valley floor. Eventually, it would have been dumped, perhaps some 20 000 years ago, out on the coastal lowlands as part of the thick boulder clay mantle. Many thousands of years later the encroaching sea released it from its earthy grip and waves set about buffeting it up and down the shore, thereby rounding it even more. Ultimately it has travelled slowly along the beach before finally coming to rest here at Black Rock.

You can ponder on this remarkable journey as you wend your way back to Criccieth. There are one or two sea-front cafés where you can purchase drinks or ice cream and perhaps browse through your collection of coloured pebbles.

# 11 Castle town: Conwy

Half a day

### Introduction

1 Conwy 🅿 **wc** 🔢
🏛 **M** (Plas Mawr) 🆙
⊘ ☕ 🔌 🏨. Early
closing Wednesday

For a complete change from mountain walking why not spend a few hours exploring the most complete and best-preserved British example of a medieval military town. It is certainly less strenuous and is particularly rewarding if you know what to look for. Also, it is a good way to while away the time on a wet, stormy day when both mountains and beaches may not be very attractive. It is equally worthwhile on a fine day, of course. The walk will take about 1 hour. Allow about 1 hour extra if you visit the castle.

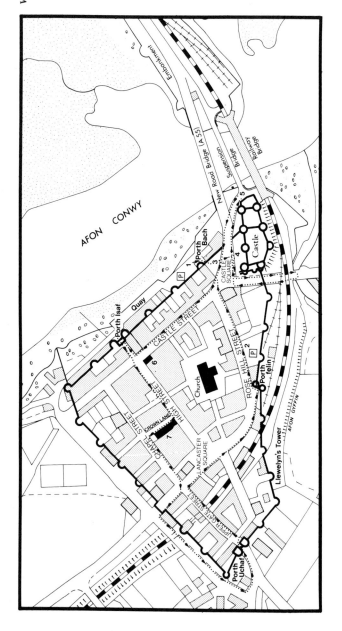

## The route

2 If this is full there is large 🅿 at Vicarage Gardens along Rose Hill Street, west of Castle Square

It is advisable to leave your car on the quayside car park for here you can best appreciate the reasons why Edward I built his castle and his fortified town at this particular spot, between the mountains and the sea.

Look first across the estuary to the Deganwy shore where two prominent hills break the skyline. These mark the site of successive Welsh castles which protected the river crossing during the 12th and 13th centuries. But the invading English king, well supplied by sea, wanted a foothold in Snowdonia itself so he chose the present site near the former Cistercian abbey of Aberconwy on the

3 Leave quay via Porth bach in town wall

western bank of the estuary. Edward had a flair for choosing good sites for his castles and Conwy is no exception. Walk up to the Castle Square and look at the narrow ridge of steeply sloping gritstone on which he constructed his fortress between 1285 and 1302. Protected to the east by the tidal waters of the Conwy and to the north, south and west by rocky cliffs, the castle's linear shape reflects the narrowness of this rocky outcrop. Now walk down the steep road southwards from the square and pass beneath the towering walls and under the railway arch. Here is the tiny valley of the Gyffin stream which acted as a natural moat on the southern flank. It was on this stream that the town's watermill was once sited and access to it was through Porth felin ('mill gate') which is the fourth tower along the town's southern wall.

Back in the Castle Square you can appreciate the massive structure of the castle, constructed almost entirely from the underlying gritstone but with a few window details and ornaments fashioned from

4 Castle: for opening times, see Appendix

a pink sandstone brought from Chester by sea. The castle is well worth a visit and the ticket office is easily accessible in the square. The view from its ramparts is superb, giving a very clear impression of the walled town you are about to explore and the way in which it nestles beneath Conwy Mountain.

After leaving the castle a short walk eastwards will allow you to examine the three bridges which span the river below the castle walls. The first bridge to be built was the suspension bridge,

5 Suspension bridge is now footbridge (NT)

superbly engineered in 1826 by who else but Thomas Telford! Until then the crossing had been made by ferry across the tide-ripped estuary, but Telford brought the main coastal road into the town by making use of a little rocky island, now virtually buried beneath the supports of the new road bridge. He had first linked the island to the eastern shore by means of an embankment, thereby narrowing the river and diverting its channel to the western bank. The second bridge, built a few years later, was the work of Stephenson who took the railway across the estuary but hid it from the suspension bridge by constructing it in tubular form, following the same principles as his more famous Britannia Bridge at the Menai Strait (see p. 32). Furthermore, its towers were designed to fit in with the crenellated castle walls. The third bridge is the largest and most modern, opened in 1956 to take the traffic load off the Telford bridge which was in a state of collapse. To avoid the original sharp bend around the castle rock the new road bridge was built out of alignment with the existing bridges and you will see something of its catastrophic consequences if you view the quay at low water. Because the river current was diverted away from the Conwy shore an enormous sand bank built up along the quay wall, leaving the fishing boats high and dry. For a few years the fishing fleet was ruined but engineers partly solved the problem by constructing a line of metal piles downstream from the bridge supports. At least the fleet can now sail out at high tide, but it is an example of how one miscalculation can interfere with the natural flow of a river to the detriment of the local people. In another sense, it was also detrimental locally when the entire volume of coastal traffic was funnelled through Conwy's narrow right-angled streets. This will finally be solved by a multi-million pound road tunnel beneath the town and the estuary, allowing Conwy to return to peace and quiet.

The route continues along Castle Street and returns to the quay at Porth Isaf. The quay is a bustling place, where you can watch the fishing fleet land its catch or the pleasure boats ply for hire. Although the town wall along the quayside is partly hidden by more recent buildings note how its stonework is more yellowish than that of the castle. This is because it is constructed in part from blocks of volcanic rock taken either from Conwy Mountain or, as some suggest, from the ruins of nearby Deganwy Castle. The town's northern wall is also built partly from the same yellowish rock but the western and southern walls are of dark Conway Castle gritstone, quarried on the site. It

(Opposite) **Conwy Castle and walled town, with the modern road bridge**

has been suggested that in medieval times there was no quay and that the tidal river Conwy washed the walls. Access to the town would have been directly from the water through the massive Porth Isaf ('lower gate'). When you re-enter the town here you will see the High Street rising straight up to Lancaster Square. Go a few yards to the cross roads and judge the ancient and modern architecture. On the opposite corner is the splended half-timbered building of Aberconwy, one of the town's oldest structures. On your left the walls of the modern telephone exchange have been built quite out of scale with that of the medieval town!

6 Aberconwy is a NT shop

As you ascend the High Street you can glimpse the ancient church on your left (behind the Castle Hotel), founded as part of the former Cistercian abbey. But your attention is probably caught by the remarkable Elizabethan mansion of Plas Mawr built in 1577. By walking up the adjacent Crown Lane you will discover the original entrance and note the great depth of this vast Tudor residence. Turning left into Chapel Street will give you a better impression of the more typical dwellings of the townsfolk; small but sturdy stone cottages with slated roofs.

7 Plas Mawr houses museum and art gallery

You may have noted how the medieval street plan, preserved in the northern part of the town, is in the form of a grid-iron. It represents the typical Norman military town plan imported from the continent and which was intended to facilitate easy defence. Every street ran straight to a wall so that in an emergency the defenders could reach the defensive towers rapidly. If you walk out through the modern northern gate (breached for the A55 trunk road) you can obtain an unbroken view of the massive town walls, punctuated by towers and guarded on this vulnerable northern side by a ditch. By following the wall southwestwards you can re-enter the town by the heavily defended Porth Uchaf ('upper gate') which was originally its main landward entrance. It faces into the mountainland along the old by-road through the Sychnant Pass (see Walk 8). Descend Upper Gate Street back to the main road where you can turn right into Lancaster Square where a statue of Llywelyn the Great dominates the scene. It is likely that this was the original market place, near to the High Street and the commercial centre of the town. But it has been claimed that the medieval market place was possibly in the Castle Square, based on the fact that

Conwy's two surviving annual fairs – the autumn Honey Fair and the spring Seed Fair – were held from time immemorial in Castle Street, until traffic drove them onto the Vicarage Car Park.

As you follow Rose Hill Street back towards the town wall you can see the way in which the railway was brought through the wall under a mock-Tudor arch, although it had to leave northwards by means of a tunnel. Conwy Station was demolished in the 1970s. If you look upwards to your right past Llywelyn's Tower, the highest part of the town comes into view near to the Upper Gate, while behind the climbing walls the silhouette of Conwy Mountain is a reminder that this eminence was the source of the town's water supply. A few yards outside Porth Uchaf is the place name Bryn ffynon ('mill spring') from where the water was led downhill in a pipeline. Tradition has it that the pipeline was once cut by the enemy, forcing the garrison to surrender. Thus, despite its apparent impregnability it is on such simple matters of physical geography that the fate of a fortified town ultimately depends. Indeed, although it has been claimed that the town was built in the shape of a Welsh harp, it was merely the lie of the land, between Gyffin stream and Conwy river, that dictated its triangular shape.

## GREAT BLACK-BACKED GULL

This is the biggest of the common gulls that breed in Britain. It occurs either solitarily or in pairs, scavenging off the beach. As a consequence this gull can frequently be seen around harbours and fishing vessels. It is also commonly found around cliffs, gliding against the updraughts of wind. Known as the butcher of the cliffs, the great black-backed gull will often pillage nests of other cliff birds, taking eggs and young alike. It has a very striking plumage, a black-grey back with a white belly and yellow bill.

# A classic railway journey:
# the Ffestiniog Railway

*Introduction*
It is something of a paradox that while British Rail have been busy closing down miles of railway track in Snowdonia, enthusiastic amateurs have been opening up stretches of new track and restoring others. The main line from Bangor to Caernarfon and thence to Afon Wen (near Pwllheli) no longer exists, nor does the line from Ffestiniog to Bala, nor that from Caernarfon to Llanberis. The rail service from Llandudno Junction to Blaenau Ffestiniog via Betws-y-Coed is under constant threat of closure. Yet North Wales has no less than six private railways of which four are in the vicinity of Snowdon. Although the Snowdon Mountain Railway is, perhaps, the most spectacular, the Ffestiniog Railway provides the most variety as it passes through constantly changing landscapes. The latter operates throughout the year; daily from March to early November but with a restricted weekend service during the winter. The journey from Porthmadog to Blaenau Ffestiniog takes an hour, so if you book a return allow half a day. For timetable and fare details phone Porthmadog (0766) 2384.

*The journey*
Like most of North Wales' light railways the Ffestiniog narrow-gauge railway started its life as a tramway to export the mineral wealth of the mountainland. In this case it was slate from the extensive mines and quarries at Blaenau Ffestiniog. While the equally large slate quarries at Bethesda and Llanberis had relatively easy overland access to the Menai Strait (at Porth Penrhyn and Porth Dinorwig, respectively) the Blaenau slate industry originally suffered from its comparative remoteness from the coast. Before the widespread introduction of road and rail transport it was imperative to use sea transport to move such a bulky item as slate. The Blaenau mines began by transporting their output by horse and cart to small wharves on the Afon Dwyryd around Maentwrog in the Vale of Ffestiniog and thence by lighter to the ocean-going ships anchored in Tremadog Bay. Once William Madocks had started to build his Glaslyn embankment, however, it was possible to construct a horse-drawn tramway all the way down from the quarries to Porthmadog quay. Thus, in 1836, the Ffestiniog Railway was born. Because the line rose from sea level to 700 feet (213 m) the gradient was such that the horses were used only for the uphill journey, with a special truck being provided for the horses to be carried on the downhill run. In 1863 steam engines were introduced and in 1865 the first passengers were carried on what was to become one of the most famous of Britain's tourist railways.

  The journey from Porthmadog starts along the famous embankment, providing magnificent views of the open sea on the one hand and on the other an unbroken view of Snowdon mirrored in the waters of the Glaslyn estuary. Ornithologists will pick out a variety of sea birds among the estuarine marshes and sandbanks, while those with cameras will find many photogenic views from either window. Although the ubiquitous car may have played a large part in causing the closure of many of Wales' branch lines, you will be pleased to be aboard a train when you see the traffic queues at the embankment toll-gate. Once past the engineering sheds, at the Boston Lodge Foundry end of the embankment, the track finally parts company with the busy trunk road as it begins to mount the low plateau surface of the Penrhyndeudraeth peninsula. Although this broad finger of land no longer has the sea washing its northern shores, because of Madocks' enclosure of Traeth Mawr, the tides still penetrate far into the Vale of Ffestiniog on its southern flank. You will see from the railway cuttings on this stretch of line that the rocks are mainly thinly bedded shales and mudstones that break down easily into relatively fertile soils. Thus, there are pocket handkerchief hayfields and sleek black cattle lining the track for the next three miles. This is the stretch where the train jogs intimately through the gardens of tiny cottages like a postman delivering mail. Near Minffordd station the mark of industry makes a brief impact on the scene as the electricity pylons march inexorably across the fields before diving down beneath the marsh in the expensive under-grounding scheme to preserve Traeth Mawr's rushy wilderness and the famous panorama of Snowdon. From this viewpoint it is rather ironic that at the very place where the lines disappear, a stone quarry in the rocky hump of Y-Garth disfigures the scene to an even greater extent than the pylons.

After Penrhyn station the track soon passes into thick woodlands of oak, ash and sweet chestnut which clothe the valley side. Here, on the wetter western slopes of Snowdonia, along the beautiful Vale of Ffestiniog, the natural deciduous woodlands of Snowdonia appear to have survived the depradations of mankind more successfully than elsewhere. However, much of this woodland was planted in the 18th and 19th centuries as part of the country estates of such landowners as the Oakley family who lived in the mansion of Plas Tan-y-bwlch (now the Snowdonia National Park Study Centre). The roof of this handsome old building, constructed by the owner of one of the largest slate quarries, will soon come into view almost vertically below the train as it steams through the woodland glades.

In order to cross the tiny 'hanging valley' at Tan-y-bwlch the engineers were forced to build the track in a large horseshoe around a thickly wooded amphitheatre. Set in the centre of the hollow is the picturesque artificial lake of Llyn Mair, which you may already have visited on Leisure drive 3. The lake waters are the haunt of black-headed gulls, little grebes and mallards and in winter of occasional whooper swans and goldeneye.

After Tan-y-bwlch station the track finally emerges from the woodlands on to the open mountainside and you will be surprised to see how high you are above the emerald green fields on the floor of the Vale. The slopes are so steep that all the settlements crouch far below on the edge of the valley floor; you can see the little grey stone village of Maentwrog at the original bridging point of the Dwyryd. The road network, too, stays on the valley floor, linking up the settlements but keeping well above the flood level.

On the rocky mountainside the track winds through banks of foxgloves and skirts marshy hollows of bog cotton and bog myrtle. At Dduallt, in order to gain height rapidly, the engineers have constructed the only railway spiral in Britain, where the line snakes back across itself before plunging into a newly constructed tunnel. All this became necessary because some years ago the next mile of line was lost beneath the waters of Tan-y-grisiau reservoir, as part of the Ffestiniog pumped storage scheme (see Drive 3). Today a new route runs above the lake shores and skirts the back of the power station. You can pick out the remains of the old trackway running into the eastern end of the lake. When you emerge at the northern end of the tunnel the scenery has changed dramatically. In place of the sylvan woods and pastoral vale is the austere, ice-scoured granite of Tan-y-grisiau. Boulder-littered hillsides, tumbling streams, bare rock faces and scrawny grassland confirm that you have now entered the true mountainland. And yet, suddenly, the train is clattering above a muddled pattern of slated roofs and stone chimneys, its whistle echoing back from the terraced cottages of a slate miners' village. Soon the gaunt, grey town of Blaenau Ffestiniog comes into view ensconced in its rugged, mountainous basin and fringed with greyish-green heaps of slaty waste, like warts on the wrinkled countenance of nature.

In Blaenau Ffestiniog you will have time to visit the new Welsh craft centre, or pay an instructive visit by bus to the nearby slate mines of Llechwedd or Gloddfa Ganol (see Appendix). If you choose either of the latter, you can make your return to Porthmadog on a later train, thereby completing a memorable day out. Alternatively, you can transfer to British Rail and continue northwards to the Conwy Valley, if you do not intend to return to Porthmadog. By alighting at Tan-y-grisau station on the Ffestiniog Railway you can explore the Ffestiniog pumped storage scheme in more detail (see Appendix).

**Tan-y-bwlch station on the Ffestiniog Railway**

# Appendix: tourist information and other places of interest

## Tourist information

Detailed tourist information and a bed booking reservation service (except where indicated *) can best be obtained from Tourist Information Centres at: Llandudno (tel.: 0492 76413); Conwy (049263 2248); Llanrwst* (0492 640604); Betws-y-Coed (06902 426); Blaenau Ffestiniog (076681 360); Harlech (076673 658); Porthmadog (0766 2981); Caernarfon (0286 2232); Llanberis (028682 765); Menai Bridge (0248 712626); Bangor (0248 52786).

Details of camping and caravan sites in and around Snowdonia may be found in: *Britain, camping and caravan sites*, British Tourist Authority, 64 St James' Street, London, SW1 (tel.: 01-499 9325). Other accommodation may be found in hotels, guest houses, youth hostels, farms, chalets and cabins. In this respect useful addresses and publications include: *Wales – where to stay*, obtainable from the Wales Tourist Board, 2 Fitzalan Road, Cardiff CF2 1UY; *Farm holiday guide*, 1985, etc. published annually by Farm Holiday Guides, 18 High Street, Paisley PA1 2BX; The Youth Hostels Association, Trevelyan House, 8 St Stephen's Hill, St Albans, Herts AL1 2DY. There are 13 Youth Hostels in the area covered by the guide. They are Bangor (OS map 115, Map Ref. 590722), Bryn Gwynant (115-641513), Capel Curig (115-726579), Ffestiniog (124-704427), Harlech (124-619308), Nant Ffrancon (115-648603), Llanberis (115-574596), Lledr Valley (115-749534), Llanrwst (116-812584), Penmaenmawr (115-737780), Pen-y-Pass (115-647556), Roe Wen (115-747721) and Snowdon Ranger (115-565550). There are two special centres: Bryn Dinas Youth Guest House in Nant Gwynant (run by The Holiday Fellowship, tel.: 01-203381) and Plas Tan-y-bwlch, near Maentwrog, Blaenau Ffestiniog (the Snowdonia National Park Study Centre) (tel.: 076685 324).

The Field Studies Council's centre at Rhyd-y-Creuau near Betws-y-Coed (tel.: 06902 494) runs such specialist courses as natural history, art and photography. Its residential accommodation is particularly suitable for school and college parties. Those interested in pursuing the more active sports of rock-climbing, skiing and canoeing may wish to stay at Plas-y-Brennin National Mountaineering Centre at Capel Curig (tel.: 06904 214/280).

Car parking in the vicinity of Snowdon may be difficult so visitors may wish to make use of the Snowdon Sherpa Bus Service.

*The Snowdon Sherpa bus service* (see accompanying map)
Designed to enable walkers to visit Snowdon more easily by leaving their cars on less crowded parks away from the mountain. Buses run regularly all round Snowdon during the summer season and will stop on request at any safe point in the national park. It provides a good opportunity to ascend Snowdon by one route (e.g. Walk 2) and descend by a different route (e.g. Walk 4). Note that you cannot park between Nant Peris and Pen-y-Gwryd except at the limited Pen-y-Pass car park. The Day Rover Ticket allows you to travel anywhere on the entire Sherpa network for a whole day and cheap family tickets (2 adults and up to 3 children) are also available.

For further information and timetable, telephone Penrhyndeudraeth (0766) 770274 or the National Park Centre at Llanberis (028682 765).

BUS INTERCHANGE
YOUTH HOSTEL
CLEARWAY : No Parking

Snowdon Sherpa bus service

## Other places of interest

### Ffestiniog hydro-electric scheme

The first pumped-storage power station built by the CEGB. From the information centre you can book tours of the power station, or take the bus up the mountain to Stwlan Dam, at an elevation of 1600 feet (487 m) on the slopes of Moelwyn Mawr. Alternatively, you can buy a permit to fish for trout in Tan-y-grisiau Reservoir. The information centre is open daily from 10.00–17.00 h at Easter weekend, and from May Bank Holiday until the end of October. There is also a café and souvenir shop (tel.: 0766 465).

### Dinorwig hydro-electric scheme

The largest pumped-storage power station in Europe, 7½ miles (12 km) east of Caernarfon and 11 miles (18 km) south of Bangor. For information on visits apply in writing to: The Public Relations Officer, CEGB (NW Region) Europa House, Bird Hall Lane, Cheadle Heath, Stockport SK3 0XA.

### Blaenau Ffestiniog Slate Industry

*Gloddfa Ganol Slate Mine* The largest slate mine in the world, where you can walk into the enormous underground chambers. You can view the blasting operations safely from an observation gallery and watch skilled workmen split the slate by traditional methods. In the mill it is possible to observe how slate blocks are processed into building stone, roofing material, hearths and ornaments. The craft shop, licensed restaurant, snack bar, natural history centre and Britain's largest narrow gauge railway collection add to the interest.

Open daily from 10.00–17.30h between Easter and the end of October (tel.: 0766 664).

*Llechwedd Slate Caverns*   An award-winning enterprise giving a choice of two underground rides. One, a conducted tour on a miners' underground tramway to see working conditions in Victorian times; the other a descent on Britain's steepest passenger railway (1 in 1.8 gradient) into the deep mine. The latter involves a walk through passages and past an underground lake. In addition, there are craft workshops, a slate mill, a smithy, a tramway exhibition, an extensive craft and souvenir shop, a licensed restaurant and café.

Open daily from 10.00–17.30 h between Easter and the end of October (tel.: 0766 664).

## Snowdon Mountain Railway
Opened in 1896 and operated entirely by steam locomotives, the railway climbs more than 3000 feet (about 1000 m) in less than 5 miles (8 km). It is Britain's only rack-and-pinion railway and carries visitors to within a few steps of Snowdon's summit at 3560 feet (1085 m). There are ample car parking facilities at Llanberis and the round trip lasts 2½ hours (including ½ hour at the summit). Trains run at frequent intervals daily from Spring Bank Holiday to early October.

Timetable and other information on 0286 870223/872331.

## Portmeirion
A fairy-tale village built in Italian-style by the late Sir Clough Williams-Ellis. It is a fantasy of pastel-coloured cottages, domes, towers and statues set in sub-tropical gardens on a wooded coastal headland in southern Snowdonia. It contains an hotel, a restaurant, shops and picnic areas.

Open daily (9.30–17.30 h) from Easter to late October. An entrance fee is charged (tel.: 0766 770457).

## Fort Belan
A private fort standing at the tip of a sandy peninsula on the western coast of Snowdonia. It has a pottery, a miniature steam railway, a maritime museum and shops, in addition to offering pleasure cruises and flights over Snowdon from its own airfield.

Open daily (10.00–17.00 h) from May to September (tel.: 0286 830220).

## Gwynedd Maritime Museum
A fine collection of photographs, models and other exhibits which records the maritime history of Snowdonia. It is situated on one of the old slate wharves of Porthmadog harbour and includes a sailing ketch built in 1909.

Open daily (10.00–18.00 h) from May to September.

## Llanberis Lake Railway
An old steam railway that once served the Dinorwig slate quarry and now provides an opportunity to ride for 4 miles along the shores of Llyn Padarn, with fine views of Snowdon. It is set in a Country Park with its woodland picnic sites, nature trail, slate museum, shops and café.

Open daily (10.30–17.00 h weekdays; 12.30–17.00 h weekends) from Easter to early October (tel.: 0286 870549).

## Bodnant Gardens

Seventy acres of terraced gardens, landscaped on the slopes of the Conwy valley and providing excellent views of eastern Snowdonia. There are fine collections of rhododendrons, camellias and magnolias set amidst specimen trees and lawns. Refreshments are available at the free car park.

Open daily (10.00–17.00 h) from Easter to late October.

## Gwydyr Castle

A well preserved and restored 15th-century castle, one of Wales' oldest residences and full of the sense of history. It stands in beautiful, wooded gardens on the western bank of the Conwy river opposite Llanrwst. Peacocks are a particular attraction among its collection of exotic birds. It has a café and a gift shop.

Open 6 days a week (closed Saturdays) from Easter to October. The nearby dower house (Gwydyr Uchaf) on the wooded hillside, is now the Forestry Commission headquarters, and houses an interesting forestry exhibition.

## Penrhyn Castle

A 19th-century neo-Norman residence built by the former slate quarry owner Lord Penrhyn amidst extensive parkland and woodland on the shores of the Menai Strait near Bangor. It provides excellent views of Snowdonia and the northern coast. It has a railway museum, exhibitions, a shop and a café.

Open daily (11.00–17.00 h) from the end of May to the end of September and (14.00–17.00 h) April to end of May and in October (all Bank Holidays 14.00–17.00 h).

## Caernarfon Castle, Conwy Castle, Harlech Castle, Segontium

The opening times of the above are as follows:

| | | |
|---|---|---|
| March–April | weekdays 9.30–17.30 h | Sundays 14.00–17.30 h |
| May–September | weekdays 9.30–19.00 h | Sundays 14.00–19.00 h |
| October | weekdays 9.30–17.30 h | Sundays 14.00–17.30 h |
| November–February | weekdays 9.30–16.00 h | Sundays 14.00–16.00 h |

## Woollen mills

The opening times are:

| | |
|---|---|
| Trefriw Mill | weekdays 8.00–12.00 h and 13.00–16.45 h |
| Trefriw Mill shop | weekdays 8.00–17.00 h |
| | Saturdays 10.00–16.00 h |
| | Sundays (July and August only) 14.00–17.00 h |
| Penmachno | 28 March–28 May Mon.–Sat. 9.00–17.30 h |
| | Sun. 13.00–17.30 h |
| | 29 May–30 June Daily 9.30–17.30 h |
| | July and August Daily 9.00–18.30 h |

# Acknowledgements

The author gratefully acknowledges the assistance of the following who helped with the preparation of this guide: Harry Walkland, who took the majority of the photographs; Dennis Hay and Maurice Parry, who lent other photographs; Duncan McCrae, who drew the illustrations and Christopher Howitt, who produced all the maps; Chris Holland and Sarah Prentice, who typed the manuscript. Above all I would like to thank my wife who drove and walked hundreds of miles in rugged terrain and in rain, wind and heatwave: without her support the guide would never have been completed.